Anonymus

The Religious Houses of the United Kingdom

Containing a short History of every Order and House compiled from official Sources

Anonymus

The Religious Houses of the United Kingdom
Containing a short History of every Order and House compiled from official Sources

ISBN/EAN: 9783742802323

Manufactured in Europe, USA, Canada, Australia, Japa

Cover: Foto ©Lupo / pixelio.de

Manufactured and distributed by brebook publishing software (www.brebook.com)

Anonymus

The Religious Houses of the United Kingdom

THE RELIGIOUS HOUSES OF THE UNITED KINGDOM.

CONTAINING A

𝔖𝔥𝔬𝔯𝔱 𝔓𝔦𝔰𝔱𝔬𝔯𝔶 𝔬𝔣 𝔢𝔟𝔢𝔯𝔶 𝔒𝔯𝔡𝔢𝔯 𝔞𝔫𝔡 𝔓𝔬𝔲𝔰𝔢.

COMPILED FROM OFFICIAL SOURCES.

LONDON: BURNS & OATES, Limited.
1887.

GUIDE

TO THE

Religious Houses of the United Kingdom.

―◆―

PART I. FATHERS.

African Missions (Society of).

Comprises Priests, Brothers, and Nuns. Founded at the request of Pius IX., for the education of missionaries for Africa. The Fathers have laboured with success amongst the idolaters of Dahomey and Ashanti, who still offer human sacrifices.

CORK, Apostolic College, Blackrock. The only house of the Society in the United Kingdom is in Ireland, where students are trained in classics; when ready for philosophy they are sent to the Mother House, which is at Lyons, France.

Andrew, St. (Institute of).

The objects of this Institute are the multiplication of missions, especially among non-

Catholic populations, and the foundation of boarding or day schools for the poor and middle classes.

BARNET, Hertfordshire, Church of Mary Immaculate and St. Gregory the Great, Union Street (1850). Schools of St. Andrew, for boarding sons of the poorer classes; of St. Pancras, for the middle classes; and of St. Peter, for ecclesiastical students. House of St. Joseph, for apprentices, who live under the same roof with the clergy, and learn their trades from Catholic masters. Hospital and Convalescent Home of St. Camillus, for boys with chronic and incurable diseases (not consumption).

ST. ALBANS, Hertfordshire, Church of SS. Alban and Stephen, London Road (1840). County Gaol and Union Workhouse.

WATFORD, Hertfordshire, Church of the Sacred Heart and St. John the Evangelist (1863).

Augustine, St., Canons Regular of Lateran of.

This Congregation of Austin Canons derives its name from the Basilica of St. John Lateran, which its members served for some centuries. The Religious date from apostolic times, live in community, take solemn vows, and follow the rule of life laid down by the

Apostles, and reduced to writing by St. Augustine.* Their churches are collegiate, and, by virtue of a Bull of Sixtus IV., enjoy all the privileges of the Basilica of St. John Lateran.

From the introduction of Christianity until the Reformation, houses of·Canons Regular were very numerous in England, and they existed in Ireland till late in the last century. Since their return to the British Isles in 1880 the Canons Regular have established three houses, which form the English Province. The General of the Congregation resides at S. Pietro in Vincoli, Rome.

BODMIN, Cornwall, Priory of St. Mary and St. Petrock, Novitiate.

MARNHULL, Blandford, Dorset, St. Mary's House, School for Postulants.

SPETISBURY,† Dorset, St. Monica's House of Studies.

* St. Augustine, the greatest of the Fathers of the Church, was born at Tagaste, in Africa, 13th Nov. 354; and died 430. His father was a pagan; his mother, St. Monica. Was converted by the latter and St. Ambrose at the age of thirty-two, after a youth of dissipation. Became Bishop of Hippo, on African border of Mediterranean, in 395. Living in common with his clergy, he laid the foundation of the Order of Canons Regular. Combated the errors of the Donatists, Manichæans, and Pelagians. Died at Hippo during its siege by the Vandals. Wrote *De Civitate Dei*, treatises on *Grace and Free Will*, *Soliloquies*, his *Confessions*, and numerous other spiritual works. His festival is observed 28th August.

† This house is at present occupied by the Brigittines, and will be shortly transferred to the Lateran Canons.

Augustinian Fathers (or Austin Friars).

Founded by St. Augustine as a Society of Hermits in Africa. Dispersed by the invasion of the Vandals in the fifth century; after their revival, they settled in England soon after the Conquest. In 1234 several branches of the Order were incorporated by Pope Innocent IV. into one Order, as to rule, habit, and habitation; and his successor, Alexander IV., confirmed this union in 1246. The present constitutions of the Order were compiled in 1278. In 1274 it was one of the four great mendicant Orders (viz. Augustinians, Dominicans, Franciscans, and Carmelites) exempted from suppression by the General Council of Lyons. A discalced branch, practising great austerities, was instituted in Portugal 1532, and soon spread over France, Spain, and Italy. This branch is governed by different Vicars-General.

The Order of the Hermits of St. Augustine has forty-two Provinces, besides those of the discalced branch, and the most recent extension of the Irish Province in Northern Queensland. At the dissolution of Monasteries in 1586 they had thirty-two houses in England and twenty-four in Ireland.

Rule—enjoining poverty, obedience, and chastity—originally given by St. Augustine to his Nuns in 423, was adopted by the Austin Friars, and took its present form in 1287.

Habit.—Originally the Friars wore only a dark-coloured or black habit like a loose-fitting tunic, with large sleeves, and girded at the waist by a black leather cincture ; a cowl (called capuche) or cape for the shoulders, with a hood attached for the head. For many centuries a white habit of similar form has been also adopted by the Order through devotion to the Blessed Virgin. The black is the more solemn form of Augustinian habit, and in Ireland is worn more generally.

The Irish Province of the Order, at the present time, has annexed to it England, Northern Queensland, and missions in Victoria, Australia. The following are the churches and Convents in England and Ireland :

LONDON, Hoxton Square, N. (1864), dedicated to Our Lady of Good Counsel, with St. Monica's Priory and extensive schools, situated in a densely populated neighbourhood in Hoxton Square, close to Shoreditch and the City Road, and was opened by Cardinal (then Monsignor) Manning, August 15th, 1864. A part of the City of London is still known as Austin Friars, where the Order possessed a Monastery founded in 1428.

DUBLIN, John Street. Originally founded in the twelfth century by Alfred de Palmer, under the title of the Augustine Priory of St. John the Baptist. The church, which has been several times rebuilt, is, together with the Convent, under the patronage of SS. Augustine and John.

BALLYHAUNIS, Co. Mayo. The Barons M'Costelloe founded a Convent for the Hermits of St. Augustine in the fourteenth century here. The ancient church continued in a state of ruin from the penal days until about ninety years ago. In 1827 the old ruined church was restored. This church and that of Fethard are the only ancient foundations in actual possession of the Order in Ireland.

CALLAN, Co. Kilkenny. Founded about the year 1480, and destroyed by Cromwell. In 1810 the present Gothic church was built. Previous to this the Friars lived in an old thatched house and chapel, a few perches from their present abode. The Convent was built in the year 1839. For many years it embraced also a college for students, and served as the novitiate of the Irish Province of the Order.

CORK, Convent, St. Augustine's, Brunswick Street, founded in the thirteenth century. At the time of the suppression it was converted into a sugar-house, and the ruins remain. The present church, between Brunswick Street and Great Georges Street, was built in 1780.

DROGHEDA, Co. Louth. Founded in the reign of Edward I. About 180 years after the general suppression a house was taken near the site of the old Convent. In 1860 the present church was built, and the Fathers now live in a new Convent erected on the site of the old one.

DUNGARVAN, Co. Waterford. Founded in 1295. The ancient church still remains. It was roofed and repaired many years ago by the secular clergy, and converted into a parish church. In 1818 the Friars established themselves in the town itself, and built a small temporary thatched chapel. The present building was begun in 1828.

FETHARD, Co. Tipperary. Founded early in the fourteenth century, and confiscated at the dissolution; but restored to the Fathers in 1820.

GALWAY. Founded in the thirteenth century on the site of the present Augustinian cemetery. At the invasion of Cromwell the Abbey was levelled to the ground.

GRANTSTOWN, Co. Wexford. Clonmines, now called Grantstown, was founded in the year 1319. The present church was built in 1830. The Convent was erected in 1811, and was for many years the novitiate of the Province.

LIMERICK. Founded in the thirteenth century by O'Brien of Limerick. A public chapel and Convent were built in 1770, in Creagh's

Lane, very near the old spot. This was the first church in Limerick in which an organ was erected. One hundred and twenty years later the Friars removed to their present abode.

NEW ROSS, Co. Wexford. Founded about 1820. About the time of George I. a thatched chapel was built for the Order on High Hill. The present church was erected in 1830.

RATHFARNHAM, County Dublin, Novitiate, Orlagh.

Attached to every Augustinian church is the Confraternity of the Sacred Cincture of the Augustinian Order. At first St. Augustine gave this cincture only to his spiritual children; but Pope Eugene IV. empowered the Order to erect a Confraternity for the admission of seculars, and this was first erected in the church of the Augustinian Fathers at Bologna in 1439.[*]

Basilian Fathers (Congregation of St. Basil).

Approved of by Pius IX. in 1863. The rules are those required for priests living in community for the greater glory of God. In pursuance of this, the members undertake every sacerdotal ministry consistent with life in common, devoting themselves more especially to the education of youth and mission work. They can remain in possession of their own property,

[*] *Leaves from St. Augustine.* Edited by T. W. Allies, M.A. (London: Burns & Oates.)

the vow of poverty for them consisting in their being obliged not to retain more than an annual income, from whatever source it may come. Each member receives every year from the Congregation a certain amount of money for clothing, books, &c.

The members wear the ordinary dress of the clergy.

They have two Colleges with several Missions in Canada and the United States, and one College in England at

DEVONPORT, Beaconfield, Novitiate and College of Mary Immaculate.

Benedictines.

Founded by St. Benedict, the Father of Western monasticism, who was born in the year 480.

The life of St. Benedict is well known.[*] The historians of an Order which counts a lineage such as this may be pardoned if they dwell with pride on the roll of Saints and learned men who have worn the black habit of St. Benedict; and in the marvellous duration of the Order, which knows no corporate body in the Western world more aged than itself (the Church excepted), and in the countless myriads of its children, may be recognised a miracle hardly less wonderful than any recorded

---

[*] See *A Sketch of the Life and Mission of St. Benedict.* By a Monk of St. Gregory's, Downside. (Burns & Oates.)

in his written life, and a testimony to the value of his Rule. For nearly 1400 years this Rule has been adapted and modified to suit the peculiar necessities of time and place by virtue of that wonderful elasticity which is not the least striking of its characteristics. Still, through every change, and as the fundamental rule of a great variety of religious bodies, its principles are preserved the same in each. They are the varied branches of the great Benedictine tree to which the self-same sap gives life and form. Perhaps what has contributed to make the Rule enduring is the principle of stability it introduced into the monastic life. This was, as Montalembert describes it, " a happy and productive innovation." Up to this time Monks had been accustomed to make no promise of remaining in the state they had entered. They had been free to leave when and how they would. St. Benedict, however, introducing greater safeguards into the time of the Monk's probation, exacted, when this was over, an oath that he would permanently abide by the result of this his deliberate choice. This legislation became the guarantee of the success and permanence of the work. "This Rule," says the great Bossuet, "is an epitome of Christianity, a learned and mysterious abridgment of all the doctrines of the Gospel, all the institutions of the Holy Fathers, and all the counsels of perfection.

Here prudence and simplicity, humility and courage, severity and gentleness, freedom and dependence, eminently appear. Here correction has all its firmness, condescension all its charm, command all its vigour, and subjection all its repose; silence its gravity, and words their grace; strength its exercise, and weakness its support."

St. Austin, the chosen instrument of Pope St. Gregory the Great for the work of England's conversion, was Prior of the Benedictine Monastery the Pope had founded in Rome. Forty Religious were made the companions of St. Austin in the work, and England became essentially Benedictine.

After the dissolution of the Monasteries in 1536 and 1539 the Benedictines were dispersed over the country. During the reign of Mary a Community was gathered together at Westminster Abbey, only to be dispersed by Elizabeth. In the persecution which followed, an effort to establish seminaries abroad was successful, and young men left their native shore to be trained for the arduous work of missionaries. The glory of the old Benedictine name and the intimate connection of the Order with England inspired many to take the Benedictine habit, in the hope that they might be allowed to resuscitate the Order. In 1601 successful application was made to the Holy See to permit the English professed in the

Cassinese Congregation to return to their country as missionaries, and a similar Brief was shortly afterwards issued to those in the Spanish Congregation; these were placed under two Superiors, who acted as the Vicars of the Cassinese and Spanish Generals. The first to enter England were Fathers Anselm Beech and Thomas Preston, who arrived in 1603 at Cisson, in Norfolk, where, at the house of Mr. Francis Wodehouse, lived Father Sigebert Buckley, who had been professed at Westminster, and was over eighty-five years of age. It was arranged, by the Superiors in Italy, that the next postulants should be clothed and professed by Father Sigebert, so that the connection with the old Congregation should remain unbroken. This was done in spite of the fact that the Gunpowder Plot threw Father Sigebert Buckley into prison. Fathers Robert Sadler and Edward Maihew, two secular priests, having been clothed by, and passed their year's noviceship with, the Italian Fathers, were professed in a cell at the Gatehouse Prison on November 21st, 1607, by Father Sigebert, then in his ninety-first year. By this profession were communicated all the rights and privileges of the old Benedictines in England, and this act of Father Buckley was confirmed by Paul V. in 1612. Shortly after, Father Buckley was released, and died at the age of ninety-three. As the Anglo-Italian Fathers had thus secured

BENEDICTINES.

the connection with the past, the Anglo-Spanish Fathers directed their attention to perpetuation in the future, by establishing, as a centre, a Monastery where Monks could be specially trained as Benedictine missionaries; and in 1605 a Monastery was founded at Douai, dedicated to St. Gregory, and soon after another, dedicated to St. Laurence, at Dieulward, in Lorraine. In 1611 a third was begun at St. Malo, called St. Benedict's, and in 1615 was founded St. Edmund's at Paris. But now difficulties arose as to the threefold jurisdiction, the Italian, Spanish, and Old English Congregations each having a Superior in England. To obviate the inconvenience arising from this, it was determined that all should be united under the name of the Anglo-Benedictine Congregation, and Pope Paul V. formally approved of its constitution and form of government in 1619; while, in order to insure its missionary character, he enacted that, besides the ordinary vows, each Monk on profession should take an oath to labour on the mission in England when called upon by his Superiors. The first General Chapter under the new constitution was held in 1621. Urban VIII. in 1633, by the Bull *Plantata*, confirmed all that had been done by his predecessor, endowed the Congregation with privileges, and enacted that it should be the only Congregation in England, commanding all other Benedictines either to join it or to return to their Monasteries. A distinctive feature in the structure of the Congregation was the separation of the missioners, who were erected into corporate bodies distinct from the Monasteries.

The Congregation is composed of distinct corporate bodies, consisting of the two missionary Provinces of Canterbury and York and the several Monasteries: over each of these is a Superior, a Prelate with regular jurisdiction, in the provinces called Provincial, in the Monasteries, Prior. Over the whole Congregation, as the Superior of the Superiors, is the President-General, who is attached to no Monastery or Province; he has the power of visitation, the control of the Superiors, can move subjects from Monastery to Mission, or from Monastery to Monastery; his power and jurisdiction are limited only by the Constitutions and Canon Law. In matters of importance he has the assistance of three Fathers, who are called "Definitors of the Regimen," who are not allowed to hold any office with jurisdiction, so that their attention may be given to the general interests of the Congregation; they also form a court of appeal.

Another distinctive feature is that of temporary Superiors, instead of Superiors for life. All officers, including the President-General, are appointed for a term of only four years, but they are eligible for reëlection. Every

BENEDICTINES.

four years the General Chapter assembles, and is composed of the Superiors, Definitors, and other officials and dignitaries. It is the supreme legislative authority and ultimate court of appeal; it controls the elections, examines the accounts of Provinces and Monasteries, receives the report of the visitations, and confirms or rejects the acts of government during the previous four years. The Provinces of Canterbury and York each form a corporate body, of which the missioners are the Community. Each Province has two "Definitors of the Province" to assist and advise the Provincial, a "Procurator" for the transaction of business matters, and holds separate funds and property. The Provincial is a Prelate in the same sense as the Prior in a Monastery, and has the same authority and jurisdiction over the missioners as if they were living in the Monastery. The Province of York comprises all the missions in the six northern counties, together with Derby, Cheshire, Nottingham, Lincoln, and Scotland; the Province of Canterbury includes the rest of England and Wales.

The Monasteries are distinct from each other, and form separate corporations, with Superior, Council, separate funds, and property. Each Monk on profession becomes affiliated to the Monastery of profession; when on the mission, and removed from the jurisdiction of the Prior, he is not absolutely detached from the Monastery; it is his home, to which he returns in infirmity or old age, or when not employed on the mission. Before the Reformation the Benedictines formed the Chapter of twelve of the old cathedrals. They chanted the Divine Office, and conducted the services of the cathedral; they had all the privileges of a Chapter of the diocese, and elected the Bishop, who nominally took the place of the Abbot, and the acting Superior of the Community was called Cathedral Prior. These titles are perpetuated by the enactment of Pope Urban VIII. The Cathedral Priories are those of Canterbury, Winchester, Durham, Ely, Worcester, Norwich, Rochester, Bath, Coventry, Peterborough, Gloucester, and Chester.

The offices are titular merely, but they give precedence and a seat in the General Chapter, and are bestowed upon eminent members of the Congregation. During the present century the Holy See has granted the dignity of titular Abbot to perpetuate the great Abbeys before the Reformation. These titles, too, give no jurisdiction, but only honour and precedence: at present they are those of Westminster, Glastonbury, St. Albans, St. Edmundsbury, Evesham, and St. Mary's, York.* By a decree of the Congregation of Propaganda, dated 21st April 1852, the Cathedral Chapter

* See *Necrology of the English Benedictines*. By Rev. T. B. Snow, M.A. (London: Burns & Oates.)

BENEDICTINES.

of the diocese of Newport and Menevia is composed of members of the English Benedictine Congregation. At present it is limited to a Cathedral Prior and five Canons residing in the Monastery adjoining the Pro-Cathedral of St. Michael and the Angels, near Hereford, and four Canons living at churches within the diocese.

The Monasteries belonging to the English Benedictine Congregation are the following:

DOWNSIDE, near Bath. St. Gregory the Great, founded in 1605 at Douai by Father Augustine Bradshaw through the munificence of Abbot Cavarel. At the French Revolution the Community was received by Sir E. Smythe at Acton Burnell, Shropshire, in 1793, where it remained till 1814, when it removed to Downside. A College is attached.

AMPLEFORTH, near York. St. Laurence, founded in 1608 at Dieulward, in Lorraine. At the French Revolution the Community obtained temporary shelter at Acton Burnell in 1794. In 1795 it removed to Birkenhead; in 1796 to Scoles, near Prescot; in 1797 to Vernon Hall; in 1802 to Parbold; and finally, towards the end of 1802, to Ampleforth. A College is attached.

DOUAI, France. St. Edmund, King and Martyr, founded in 1615 in Paris. At the

Revolution in 1793 the Community was imprisoned in the Monastery itself for fourteen months. In 1796 the Monastery was restored, and in 1804 the Monks were again expelled. In 1823 they were reëstablished in the old buildings of St. Gregory's at Douai. A College is attached.

BELMONT, Hereford, General Novitiate and Tyrocinium. St. Michael and the Angels, founded at Belmont in 1859. A decree of the Holy See ordered a common Novitiate, and that at the end of the year of noviceship the young Monks, after their simple profession, should remain three years in a house of studies before returning to their Monastery for solemn profession. This Monastery, attached to the Benedictine diocese of Newport and Menevia, was erected to carry out the designs of the Holy See. The Prior is a "Cathedral Prior."

The following missions are filled by priests who are Monks of one or other of the above Monasteries:

Province of Canterbury.

ABERGAVENNY, Co. Monmouth, Church of St. Michael.

ACTON BURNELL, Shrewsbury, Church of St. Peter (1845-6).

BATH, St. John's Priory and Church, South Parade. Mission Church of St. Benedict (1857),

BENEDICTINES.

Downside. Served from St. Gregory's Monastery.

BRIDGEND, Co. Glamorgan, Church of St. Mary (1856).

BONHAM, Stourton, Bath.

BUNGAY, Co. Suffolk, Church of St. Edmund (1822).

CHELTENHAM, Somerset Place, St. Gregory's Priory.

CHIPPING SODBURY, Gloucestershire, Church of St. Lawrence (1838).

CLEHONGER, near Hereford.

COUGHTON, Redditch, Church of SS. Peter and Paul and St. Elizabeth (1857). This mission and chaplaincy, belonging to the Throckmorton family, has been served by priests of the Anglo-Benedictine Congregation for two hundred years.

COVENTRY, Warwickshire, Church of the Blessed Sacrament, and St. Osburg's Priory.

DOWLAIS, Glamórganshire, Church of St. Iltutus (1844-6).

HEREFORD, Church of St. Francis Xavier (1837-9).

KEMERTON, Tewkesbury, Gloucestershire, Church of St. Bennet (1843).

MAESTEG, Glamorganshire, Church of Our Lady and St. Patrick.

MALVERN, GREAT, Church of St. Joseph.

MALVERN, LITTLE, Church of St. Wulstan.

MERTHYR TYDVIL, Glamorganshire, Church of St. Mary.

NEWNHAM PADDOX, Lutterworth, Church of the Sacred Heart. Belongs to the Bishop of Birmingham, but is at present served by a priest of the Anglo-Benedictine Congregation, chaplain to Lord Denbigh.

REDDITCH, Warwickshire, Church of Our Lady of Mount Carmel (1834).

STRATFORD-ON-AVON, Warwickshire, Church of St. Gregory the Great (23rd October 1866).

STUDLEY, Redditch, Church of St. Mary (1851-1853).

SWANSEA, Glamorganshire, St. David's Priory, St. Joseph's Priory, General Infirmary, Fever Hospital, Gaol, Union Workhouse, four Poor Schools.

WEOBLEY, Herefordshire, Church of St. Thomas of Hereford (1834).

WOOTTON-WAWEN, Henley-in-Arden, Warwickshire, Church of Our Blessed Lady and St. Benedict (1814).

Province of York.

ABERFORD, Leeds, Church of St. Wilfrid (1786).

AIGBURTH, Grassendale, Liverpool, Church of St. Austin (1838).

BARTON-ON-HUMBER, Church of St. Augustine.

BEDLINGTON, Northumberland, Church of St. Bede (1876).

BIRTLEY, Durham, Church of St. Joseph (1696).

BLYTH, Northumberland, Church of Our Lady and St. Wilfrid (1861).

BRINDLE, Preston, Church of St. Joseph.

BROWNEDGE, Preston, Church of St. Mary.

CLAYTON GREEN, Chorley, Lancashire, Church of St. Bede.

CLEATOR, Carnforth, Cumberland, Church of Sacred Heart of Our Lady (1853-72).

COWPEN, Northumberland, Church of St. Cuthbert (1841).

EASINGWOLD, Yorkshire, Church of St. John, (1830).

EGREMONT, Carnforth, Cumberland, Church of St. Bridget (1878).

FRIZINGTON, Carnforth, Cumberland, Church of St. Joseph (1875).

GARFORTH, Leeds, Church of St. Joseph (1883). Served from Aberford.

GOOSNARGH, Preston, Lancashire, Church of St. Francis.

HARRINGTON, Workington, Cumberland, Church of St. Mary (1874).

HINDLEY, Wigan, Lancashire, Church of St. Benedict.

KNARESBRO', Yorkshire, Church of St. Mary (1797).

LEE HOUSE, near Preston, Church of St. William (1788).

LEYLAND, Preston, Church of St. Mary (1854).

LIVERPOOL, St. Mary's Priory (1844-5), 12 St. Paul's Square; St. Peter's Priory (1788, 1818), Seel Street; St. Anne's Priory (1843-46), Edge Hill; St. Augustine's Priory (1848-9), Great Howard Street.

MARYPORT, Cumberland, Church of St. Patrick (1847).

MORPETH, Northumberland, Church of St. Robert of Newminster.

NETHERTON, Great Crosby, Liverpool, Church of St. Bennet (1793).

PARBOLD, Wigan, Church of Our Lady and All Saints (consecrated 1884).

SCARISBRICK, near Ormskirk, Lancashire, Church of St. Mary (1812).

WALTON-LE-DALE, Preston, Church of St. Patrick.

WARRINGTON, Lancashire, St. Alban's (1823); St. Mary's Priory (1877).

WARWICKBRIDGE, Carlisle, Church of St. Mary (founded before 1720; 1841).

WHITEHAVEN, Cumberland (Coach Road), Church of St. Begh (1834, 1868).

WOOLTON - MUCH, Liverpool, St. Mary's (1765-1860).

WORKINGTON, Cumberland, Priory of Our Lady and St. Michael (1811).

WRIGHTINGTON HALL, Wigan, Lancashire, Church of St. Joseph.

Besides the above Monasteries, Colleges, and Missions belonging to the Anglo-Benedictine Congregation, there are three other branches of the great Benedictine Order in England and Scotland, whose houses are:

RAMSGATE, Kent, Church, Monastery, and College of St. Augustine: founded in 1856, is a Priory of the Cassinese Congregation of the Order of St. Benedict. This Congregation, which has its principal seats in the Monasteries founded in the sixth and seventh centuries by St. Benedict at Subiaco and Monte Cassino, in Italy, was in part reformed by the late Abbot, Peter Casaretto, who, by command of Pope Pius IX., introduced it into England and other countries of Western Europe. The only religious house in England in any way connected with St. Augustine's is Buckfast Abbey. The Benedictines of Ramsgate unite the more austere interpretation of the Rule of St. Benedict in regard to solitude, penance, and prayer, with educational and missionary work. The College directed by the Fathers adjoins their Monastery.

MARGATE, Church of SS. Austin and Gregory, Victoria Road (1804). This mission has been served for the last thirty years by the above Cassinese Fathers, whose Provincial resides at Ramsgate. The foundation of a new church, with annexed Priory, at Margate, is in immediate contemplation.

BUCKFAST, near Buckfastleigh, Devon, St. Mary's Abbey. Founded in 1137 by Ethelwerd, son of William de Pomeroy; affiliated to Clairvaux (Cistercian) in 1138; again occupied by Benedictine Monks belonging to the Cassinese Congregation of the Primitive Observance, from Pierre-qui-Vire, near Avallon, on October 28th, 1882. First stone laid of the restored south cloister, October 7th, 1884; new building being raised on the ancient foundations. The south side of the restored Abbey was opened on April 27th, 1886.

ERDINGTON, Birmingham, SS. Thomas and Edmund of Canterbury. A Priory belonging to the Beuron Congregation. The Abbey of Beuron, for some time empty, owing to the May Laws, has been restored to the Order this year.

FORT AUGUSTUS, St. Benedict's Abbey. This Monastery, which formerly belonged to the English Benedictine Congregation, has, since January 1883, been immediately subject to the jurisdiction of the Holy See. It is finely situated at the head of Loch Ness, almost in the centre of the great waterway formed by the Caledonian Canal and a chain of natural lakes which connects Fort William with Inverness. The buildings of the Monastery occupy the site of the old military fort originally constructed in 1715, and rebuilt in 1725 by General Wade. The fort was the centre of great activity in the rebellion of 1745, and after the battle of Culloden was for some time the head-quarters of Cumberland's victorious army. It was subsequently used as a barrack, but in course of time was dismantled, and was finally sold, in 1867, by Government to the late Lord Lovat. Some years later, the Marquis of Bute offered the sum of 5000*l.* to the English Benedictine Congregation, for the purpose of founding a Monastery in Scotland. Various sites were suggested for the proposed foundation, but it was finally decided to accept the munificent offer of Lord Lovat, who presented the site of Fort Augustus, together with the old fort and sixteen acres of ground. The foundations of the new buildings were laid in September 1876, the Marquis of Ripon, Lord Lovat, and others taking part in the proceedings. The arduous work of collecting funds for the building and establishing the new foundation

on a solid basis was intrusted to Dom Jerome
Vaughan, a Canon of Newport and Menevia;
and with such zeal and success did he prose-
cute his task, that in 1878 the buildings (which
were erected by Mr. Hansom) were sufficiently
advanced to permit of the commencement of
monastic observance and the opening of the
College attached to the Monastery. By 1880
the buildings, with the exception of the church,
were finished; and in September of the same
year, being the fourteenth centenary of St.
Benedict, the completed Monastery was dedicated to the service of God. For some time
previous to the date of the severance of Fort
Augustus from the English Congregation there
had been a strong desire among various members to see a renovation in the observance of
monastic discipline, which was greatly impeded
by the claims of the numerous missions served,
and the consequent claim on the Monasteries
of the Order in England. A Papal Visitor was
appointed in 1881, to inquire into the question,
and it was decided to take independent action
with regard to Fort Augustus. Accordingly,
a petition was submitted to the Holy Father,
signed by the Primate and other members of
the Scottish Hierarchy, and by the founder and
chief benefactors of the Monastery, praying
for separation from the English Congregation.
His Holiness was pleased to accede to the
prayer, and by a Brief he raised the Monastery

to the rank of an Abbey immediately subject to the Holy See.

The buildings of the Abbey consist of the Monastery proper, which has accommodation for about forty Monks; the Abbey School, adapted for seventy pupils; and the Hospitium, in which guests are received and entertained, according to the precept of the Rule, and which also offers accommodation to about a dozen young men, who are prepared for the army, civil service, and other public examinations. Besides these buildings, which occupy three sides of the square formed by the remains of the old fort, there is also a Scriptorium, or School of Art, in which drawing, painting, and architecture are taught and studied, and containing a small printing-press. The quadrangle is surrounded by cloisters, erected by Mr. Pugin in the Early Decorated style, and perhaps not surpassed by anything of the kind in modern work. The present church is a temporary structure of wood, which it is intended shortly to replace by a permanent church. Attached to the Abbey there is a large and scattered parish, containing some four or five hundred Catholics, and served for the present by a secular priest. The principal occupation of the Monks is the carrying on of the Abbey School, literary work, giving retreats to the clergy and others, and, above all, in the solemn and exact performance of the Liturgy of the Church. Mass is sung daily, and on the principal festivals the Divine Office is carried out with all possible splendour and solemnity.

The *Habit* of the Monks of Fort Augustus consists of a black serge tunic, with leather belt, black scapular and hood; likewise a black cowl, worn in choir. They receive the coronal tonsure. The details of their monastic observance are founded to a great extent on that of the Congregation of Béuron, which is well known on the Continent as one of the youngest and at the same time most fervent, exact, and flourishing branches of the Benedictine Order. The Monks of Fort Augustus have recently brought out an edition of the Rule of St. Benedict, with an English translation and explanatory notes (Burns & Oates).

Capuchins.

These are a branch of the Order of Friars Minor instituted by St. Francis of Assisi, and originated in 1525 by a Friar of the Franciscan Observantines, Father Matthew of Bassi. The object of its institution was to restore the primitive regular observance of the Rule of St. Francis; and it is the last reform that has taken place in the Franciscan Order. The Franciscan Capuchins also resumed the shape of the habit as worn by St. Francis, a coarse robe, and a long hood without the *cappa*, which, together with the smaller hood, was introduced into the Order of Friars Minor after the death of St. Francis. It is from the fact of wearing the long capuch or hood that the Capuchins derive their name. The first General Chapter of the Capuchins was held at Alvacina in 1529, when Clement VII. constituted them a distinct branch of the Franciscan Order, under a Vicar-General chosen from their own body. In 1619 Urban VIII. gave the Franciscan Capuchins a Minister-General. The Capuchin Order numbers eight thousand members, about one thousand of whom are engaged on the foreign missions.

They first came into England in 1630, being brought over from France by Henrietta, Queen of Charles I.; established in Somerset House. In 1669 they were expelled from the kingdom. They returned to England in 1850, and for a time dwelt in London. In 1852 the present Earl of Denbigh, then Viscount Fielding, invited them to Pantasaph, to take possession of the church he had just built. After this other houses were established; and in 1873 the Order in England was properly established as a canonical Province, under the patronage of St. Laurence of Brindisi.

The work of the Franciscan Capuchins is principally to assist secular priests by giving missions, retreats, sermons, &c. Besides this they have in England the care of parishes, which are attached to each of the Monasteries.

The Order has no educational establishment in England, but educates its own members who aspire to the priesthood. At present Pantasaph, which is the Mother House of the Order in England, is the House of Novitiate and of the study of philosophy. Yet it is by no means against the statutes of the Order to conduct educational establishments, and, in fact, in many of their Provinces the Capuchins have colleges for the education of youth.

Being a mendicant Order, it depends entirely for its subsistence upon the alms of the faithful in those things which cannot be obtained by the industry of the Friars themselves. Considering the circumstances under which the mendicant Orders are placed in England, the Capuchins have received permission from the Holy See to possess property for the time being.

CHESTER (Grosvenor Street), Church of St. Francis (1858).

CRAWLEY, Sussex (Study House), Church and Monastery of St. Francis (1858); Cemetery.

ERITH (West Street), Kent, Church of St. Fidelis (1870).

PANTASAPH, Church and Monastery of St. David. Founded by Lord Denbigh, and was begun before his reception into the Church; but after this event it and the ground attached were handed over to the Capuchins. The church, dedicated to St. David, Patron of Wales, is a solid and noble stone structure, with a fine open nave and one side aisle. The Monks themselves have wrought with their own hands the altars of the Sacred Heart and St. Francis, and the Psalter stand in the choir. In the grounds of the Monastery the Stations of the Cross are a distinguishing feature. These occur at intervals of one hundred and fifty yards, along a road leading up the side of a mountain, on the summit of which stands a massive Calvary, which is visible for many miles.

LONDON: EAST DULWICH, S.E. (Five Elms, Lordship Lane), St. Anthony of Padua (1879); Peckham, Lower Park Road, S.E., Church of Our Lady of Seven Dolours (1855).

NUNEATON, Co. Warwick, Our Lady of the Angels (1880).

PONTYPOOL, Co. Monmouth, Monastery of St. Alban (1859).

CORK, Convent and House of Studies, Holy Trinity, Charlotte Quay.

DUBLIN, Convent of St. Mary of the Angels, Church Street.

KILKENNY, Capuchin Friary and Seraphic School, Walkin Street.

ROCHESTOWN, Co. Cork, St. Joseph's Capuchin Monastery and Novitiate.

Carmelites.

This Order traces its origin and name to Mount Carmel in Syria, where, according to the tradition received by the Church, the Prophet Elias united his disciples in a religious corporation nine centuries before the Christian era. These hermits continued in existence till the advent of our Lord, and were known by the various names of Rechabites, Sons of the Prophets, or Essenes. In the fourth century, John Nepos, forty-fourth Bishop of Jerusalem, gave them their first Rule; in 1207, at the request of Brocard, their Prior-General, this was more precisely defined by Albert, Patriarch of Jerusalem, and confirmed by Pope Honorius in 1238. Introduced into Europe by St. Louis in 1238. Came to England in 1240, and in course of time obtained forty houses, the extension of the Order having been greatly promoted by St. Simon Stock, who was elected sixth General at a General Chapter held at Aylesford in 1245. This holy man received from the Blessed Virgin the celebrated privilege of the scapular, at Cambridge, on the 16th July 1251. Introduced in the middle of the thirteenth century into Ireland, where they had twenty-five houses—the one in Whitefriars Street, Dublin, having been founded in 1274. Was one of the four mendicant Orders permitted to continue by the General Council of Lyons in the same year. The Order is chiefly contemplative, but does

CARMELITES.

not exclude active works, though these are of secondary importance. It is divided into Calced, Discalced, and Tertians. The Discalced Carmelites are a reform introduced in the sixteenth century by St. Teresa, assisted by St. John of the Cross. These do not teach; but the Calced have both day and boarding schools, while the Tertians are laymen, of whom some live in community. The first oratory in honour of our Lady was erected in the apostolic times by the Carmelites; and the original Monastery still exists on Mount Carmel, where the Monks guard the grotto and fountain of the Prophet Elias. The English Province was restored in 1862.

Habit.—Brown, with white cloak, and a hood. Owing to the white cloak, the Carmelites were also called "White Friars"—a name still retained in that part of London lying between Fleet Street and the Thames, where they had a Convent, and where the church of Whitefriars was founded by Sir Richard Grey in 1241.

(Discalced). — LONDON: KENSINGTON, 47 Church Street, W., Church of Our Lady of Mount Carmel and St. Simon Stock. Cardinal Wiseman, wishing to establish a Monastery of Carmelites in London in 1862, asked the Superior-General in Rome to let him have the celebrated Père Hermann to carry out the projected foundation. Père Hermann arrived in London on the 6th August 1862, and on the 15th of October (Feast of St. Teresa), in the same year, the Convent and chapel were opened in a little house belonging to the Nuns of the Assumption, in Kensington Square.

The Community took possession of its present house in Church Street, Kensington, on October 17th, 1863. On the 17th of July 1865, Cardinal Manning blessed and laid the foundation-stone of the present church, which was opened on the Feast of Our Lady of Carmel, 16th July 1866. Père Hermann founded here the same devotion of the nocturnal adoration of the Blessed Sacrament every week, which he had already instituted in Paris, and there is Exposition of the Blessed Sacrament every second Thursday of the month.

WINCANTON, Somersetshire, Friary of St. Luke.

DUBLIN, St. Teresa's, Clarendon Street.

DONNYBROOK, DUBLIN, St. Mary's, Morehampton Road.

LOUGHREA, Co. Galway, Monastery (The Abbey) and Novitiate. Notwithstanding the alienation of its revenues at the dissolution, the Monastery at Loughrea, founded in 1300, has preserved a continuous succession in its members. Owing to dilapidation, a chapel and an adjoining dwelling-house were erected in 1785; the former being rebuilt on a more extensive scale in 1816, and the latter in 1829, at an expenditure of four thousand pounds, defrayed from the funds of the establishment and from subscriptions, liberally contributed to by the Clanricarde family, on whose estate the Monastery is situated.

(Calced). — DUBLIN, Whitefriars Street, founded 1274 by Sir Robert Bagot. Suppressed at the dissolution, it was reëstablished in 1825. Intermediate day-schools.

KILDARE, White Abbey, founded between 1267 and 1290. In the sixteenth century the Convent and church were destroyed; but the Friars remained in the neighbourhood, and when the dawn of religious freedom arose, they secured a portion of the old site, on which they built a church and Convent. In 1884 was laid the first stone of the present Abbey, on the very foundation of the ancient White Abbey, and this church was modelled as far as possible on the same style as the old structure. A high-class classical school is at present attached to the Abbey.

KNOCKTOPHER, Co. Kilkenny. The old Abbey, which is only a few paces from the present site, was founded 1280, and destroyed by Cromwell. The present Convent has had for many years an extensive school. In consideration of the great success of the teaching of the Carmelite Fathers, his Holiness the Pope, half a century ago, established a university here.

KINSALE, Co. Cork. Founded in the fourteenth century. Intermediate day-schools.

MOATE, Co. Westmeath. Founded in the fourteenth century.

TERENURE COLLEGE, near Dublin. Novitiate and house of studies. A boarding-school for boys is attached to this house.

Carthusians.

Founded in 1084 by St. Bruno of Cologne, Canon of Reims, who had withdrawn with six companions into the desert of Chartreuse, among the rugged mountains near Grenoble, and in the vicinity of whose cell the monastery of La Grande Chartreuse—the residence of the General of the Order—was built in 1134. The rules, which are original, but embrace some of the constitutions of St. Benedict, were first reduced to writing in 1110, and confirmed by Pope Alexander III. about 1174, and were, after subsequent additions, compiled into a complete code in 1581, and approved by Innocent XI. in 1688. The Order was introduced into England about 1180, and the first house at Witham, in Somerset, was built by St. Hugh of Lincoln, who was its Prior, until he became Bishop of Lincoln. Another house was founded in London by Sir William Marney in 1371, on the site of the present Charterhouse, a corruption of the word Chartreuse. In all there were eleven

Monasteries in England. All the houses of the Order were placed under the Prior of the Grande Chartreuse in 1141 at the first General Chapter of the Order. This Prior was St. Autelme, afterwards Bishop of Belley, who died in 1178. They were expelled from France, and their fine library at the Grande Chartreuse destroyed in 1794, but were restored in 1815, when they succeeded in recovering possession of La Grande Chartreuse. In some respects, such as the solitude, length of night office, and total abstinence from flesh-meat, this is the most austere of all the Orders.

Rule enjoins solitude and silence, frequent fasting, entire abstinence from meat, singing of the Divine Office, meditation, study, and manual labour. They take a walk together outside the Monastery once a week, and a little recreation in common on certain festivals.

PARKMINSTER, Partridge Green, Steyning, Sussex, Convent, Chartreuse of St. Hugh. Since the martyrdom of the venerable John Houghton, Prior of the London Charterhouse, with several of his Monks, in 1535, followed by the total suppression of the Order in this country, little is known about the fate of the various Communities, except that of Sheen, Surrey. The Carthusians, driven from this Monastery, retired to Bruges. In Queen Mary's reign, Father Chauncey, who had belonged to the London Charterhouse, left Bruges with several others, and came back to London in June 1555. In 1556 they recovered their ancient Monastery at Sheen, and Father Chauncey was made Prior. Driven again from England in 1559, they returned to Bruges, which they were obliged to leave in consequence of the tumults raised by the Calvinists. They then went to Douai; and thence to the Charterhouse of Louvain, 1578-90. Father Chauncey died at Paris in 1581, and Father Walter Pitts was the next Prior. The Community removed to Antwerp in 1590, and thence to Mechlin in 1591. In 1626 they went to Nieuport, Flanders, remaining there till their final suppression in 1783; their numbers were then three Monks and two lay Brothers. This was the only English Community of religious men who had continued without dispersion from the reign of Queen Mary. The last of the English Carthusians was Prior Williams, who died at Malvern, in the strict observance of his Rule, in 1797. From this date until 1850, when an Irish priest took the habit at Florence, it is doubtful whether there was an English-speaking Carthusian. In 1863 the General of the Carthusian Order, Father Charles M. Saisson, sent two Monks to England (one of whom was the said Irish priest), in consequence of a proposal made by the Right Rev. Dr. Clifford, Bishop of Clifton, to establish a house of the Order in his diocese. This journey, however, came to nothing. Another deputation from the Grande Chartreuse in 1872 came to a better end, for it resulted in the purchase of the site for the present beautiful Monastery of St. Hugh's, Parkminster, Sussex. The foundation-stone of this house was laid by Dr. Danell, Bishop of Southwark, in 1877. The consecration of the church took place on May 10th, 1883, by Bishop Coffin. This is by far the largest monastic building in England, though not as yet the most numerous Community. There are at present twenty choir Monks (seventeen of whom are priests) and ten lay brethren.

Charity, Fathers of (The Institute of).

Institute of Charity, founded in 1828 by the Abbate Antonio Rosmini-Serbati at Domodossola, in Northern Italy. Approved by Gregory XVI. in 1838. Has for its end the sanctification of its members by means of the exercise of every work of charity, spiritual, intellectual, or corporal, under the direction of obedience. Came to England first in the summer of 1835, at the request of Bishop Baines, who had invited them to form part of the teaching staff of the College at Prior Park, Bath, Father Gentili being the first Superior.

CARDIFF, Church of St. Peter (1861). This church was built by the Fathers of Charity.

The church was opened in the year 1861, the presbytery being added at a later period. Up to three years ago the whole town of Cardiff, with the other churches, was under the care of the said Fathers. In order to enable the Bishop to make Cardiff his principal seat, the Fathers of Charity retired from the other churches, and St. Peter's alone remains in their charge. The mission possesses very good schools—boys, girls, and infants; as also a young ladies' school, taught by the Sisters of Providence of the Institute of Charity.

GLEN TROPHY, near Abergavenny, Monmouthshire.

LONDON, 14 Ely Place, Holborn, E.C.; Church of St. Etheldreda (1290; 1876), Ely Place; City of London Union.

This church is remarkable as being the last church in which Mass was said after the schism of England from the Holy See, and it is the first in which the Catholic rites have been restored. It is a gem of mediæval architecture, having been built about 1280. It is a specimen of the English development in the form of a chapel of that well known in its French development in the Sainte Chapelle in Paris, which it surpasses in the grandeur of its west windows, although it wants the elegant finish of the elaborate stone vaulting of its French contemporary. St. Etheldreda's was formerly the domestic chapel of the Bishops of Ely. During the reigns of Edward VI. and Elizabeth the Palace was let to the Spanish Ambassador, and then the chapel was used for Catholic worship. Afterwards the Anglican service was used in it up to the time when it passed into the hands of the Fathers of Charity. About a century ago the Bishop of Ely got an Act of Parliament to enable him to sell his London Palace, which became secular property. About ten years ago the property again came to be sold, and was bought by the Fathers of Charity. This church is also interesting, since it contains some of the relics of St. Etheldreda beneath the high altar. These were discovered about a century ago in pulling down a farmhouse in Sussex belonging to the Duke of Norfolk, a part of which had been used as a priests' hiding-place in the days of persecution. It is thought that these relics of the Saint, which came originally from Ely, were preserved in the church named after her in London. There is a large Community house attached to the church.

LOUGHBOROUGH, Co. Leicester, Church of St. Mary (1835).

MARKET-WEIGHTON, Yorkshire, Church of St. William (1863); Reformatory School for Boys.

NEWPORT, Monmouth, Church of St. Mary (1840).

RATCLIFFE COLLEGE, near Leicester; College of the Immaculate Conception (1847). Has been for more than forty years a well known place of education. It is intended for those who find the larger Colleges too expensive, but who wish for their children a thoroughly refined, Christian, classical, and commercial education. The sons of those who were educated at Ratcliffe are to be found among the pupils, and many priests as well secular as of the Order of Charity have been there educated, as well as gentlemen now in the higher walks of political and business and professional life. Professed House of the Institute of Charity, founded in 1852. For many years used as Scholasticate and Novitiate until the year 1881, when the Novitiate was transferred to The Mount, Wadhurst, Sussex. To the Scholasticate has recently been added a Juniorate, into which the sons of respectable parents are received and prepared for entrance into the Novitiate. Age of admission, twelve to sixteen. A public church is attached, under the charge of the Fathers, with boys' and girls' schools, the former directed by the Brothers of the Order, the latter by the Sisters of Providence of Loughborough.

RUGBY, Warwickshire, St. Marie's Church (1847).

WADHURST, Sussex, Novitiate House, The Mount (1881). A beautiful Gothic building in the midst of wooded grounds, designed by Mr. Bernard Whelan.

CLONMEL, Co. Tipperary, Industrial School of St. Joseph (1884). A beautiful Gothic structure, built by Count Moore, and presented to the Fathers of Charity.

UPTON, Co. Cork, St. Patrick's Reformatory School (1859). A grand institution, doing much good, and in high esteem with the citizens of Cork.

Cistercians.

Founded in 1098 by St. Robert of Molesme as a reform of the Benedictine Order, assisted by an Englishman, St. Stephen Harding—for if St. Robert of Molesme was its first founder, St. Stephen was its great organiser, who established in the new Order of Citeaux the annual Chapter, in which the Abbots of all the Monasteries were to meet together to maintain discipline and reform abuses, and the system of reciprocal visitation between the Abbeys themselves. So simple and yet so admirable was Stephen's plan that not only Cluny itself, but even later Congregations, such as Dominicans, Franciscans, and other religious bodies, more or less adopted it or profited by it; and in the Fourth Lateran Council under Innocent III. the General Chapters of Citeaux were expressly brought forward as a model for the revival of monastic life. Evil days fell on Citeaux until the arrival of St. Bernard in 1113. In the second Chapter-General, held in 1119, St. Stephen put forth certain statutes to which he gave the name of the "Chart of Charity," and which "Chart of Charity" was solemnly approved by Pope Calixtus II. Various reforms have in the course of centuries been introduced, the most celebrated being that of the Abbé Armand de Rancé in 1663, and known as that of La Trappe. Introduced into England in 1128, their first house was at Waverley, in Surrey, and at the dissolution they had 101 houses in England and Wales. Reëstablished in the United Kingdom, in Ireland, in 1833.

Rule.—The Benedictine, in its primitive austerity, including prayer and manual labour, and diet confined to bread and vegetables cooked in water.

Habit.—White tunic and black scapular for their ordinary and working dress, and over this, in the choir and the house, the white cowl, which covers the whole person. The lay brethren wear dark brown tunic and scapular, with hood and mantle.

CAPPOQUIN, Co. Waterford, Abbey of Mount Melleray. Founded in 1833 by a colony of Trappist Monks from the Abbey of Melleraye, France. Driven from France by the Revolution of 1830, they first settled at Rathmore, in Kerry. The Community of Melleraye in France counted nearly 200 members, of whom many were Irish, and the blow aimed at its destruction was very severe; but the result was the restoration in Ireland of the venerable Cistercian Order after an exile of three centuries.

At present (1886) the number of members in community of Mount Melleray is over eighty, about one-third of whom are priests. There is a classical seminary under the care of some of the priests; it has about 120 students, chiefly ecclesiastical. There is also a large primary school, for the gratuitous education of the sons of the peasantry in the surrounding district. Neither of these schools has ever received any Government aid. At the Guest-house priests and gentlemen are received who wish to spend a few days or weeks in retreat. A house, in charge of a matron, is provided for ladies at a short distance from the Monastery.

LEICESTER, St. Bernard's Abbey, Coalville. Founded in 1837 from Mount Melleray, Waterford, by the aid of Mr. Ambrose de Lisle Phillips, of Grace Dieu Manor, Leicestershire, and of John Earl of Shrewsbury. The building was intrusted to Augustus Welby Pugin, the famous architect, whose services were to a considerable extent rendered gratuitously; and to the honour of the Monks be it recorded that

the stone was got from their own ground, and
that they worked at the erection of their Abbey
untiringly, unflinchingly, and with the same
commendable and noble spirit that had actuated
their predecessors, "the Monks of old." The
guest-quarters are situated partly in the gatehouse and partly in the adjacent buildings.
They consist of reception-rooms for visitors in
general, and bedrooms for such strangers as
may come to the Abbey either for a retreat or
on a visit. The house for the entertainment
of the poor is to the right of the porter's lodge
on entering. Here come the hungry, the needy,
and the afflicted of all ages and creeds; nor
need any one fear to be turned away by the
kind-hearted Brother who is expressly appointed
to wait upon and serve them.*

ROSCREA, Co. Tipperary, Mount St. Joseph
Abbey. Founded from Mount Melleray Abbey
on March 17, 1878, on a property the gift of
Count Arthur Moore, of Mooresfort, Tipperary.
The foundation-stone of the new Gothic church
was laid on May 23, 1879; the church itself
was solemnly blessed on September 18, 1881.
From being a Priory, the Monastery was raised
to the rank of Abbey in December 1885, by a
decree of his Holiness Leo XIII., and by a subsequent Brief of March 16, 1886.

* For further particulars see *Guide to the Abbey of Mount
St. Bernard*, by Llewellyn Jewitt, F.S.A. (Leicester: John &
Thomas Spencer.)

Dominicans, or Friars Preachers.[*]

Founded in 1215 at Toulouse by St. Dominic. Accompanying his Bishop to France, he devoted himself to the conversion of the Albigensian and other heretics, for which object he instituted the Order of Friars Preachers, their mission being to preach and teach. Some time before this (about 1208) he had revealed to him the devotion of the Rosary of the Blessed Virgin. This is one of the four mendicant Orders allowed by the General Council of Lyons in 1274. They have also a Third or Tertiary Order, some of whom live in community, and others are lay persons of both sexes, married and single, living in the world.

Rule.—Based on that of St. Augustine, enjoining silence, fasting, poverty, and other mortifications.

Habit.—At first St. Dominic retained his habit as a Canon Regular of St. Augustine, but changed this in 1219 to a white tunic and capuce with a scapular, over which is worn, when going abroad, a black cappa and capuce; a leather girdle, with a rosary or chaplet suspended from the waist.

The Dominicans first came to England in 1221. At their house in Holborn two General Chapters were held in 1250 and 1263, the latter attended by St. Thomas Aquinas. In 1276 they

[*] *Life of St. Dominic.* By Père Lacordaire (translated). (London: Burns & Oates.)

obtained the award of a large piece of ground between Ludgate and the Thames, which from them acquired the name, still preserved, of Blackfriars, as the Monks were called in England, from their black cappa. This house was on the site of the *Times* office in Printing House Square, and here were held the General Chapters of 1314 and 1335.

At the Reformation the Dominicans possessed fifty-two Priories and two subsidiary houses in England and Wales, and there was one Priory of Sisters of the Second Order. The Dominican Province was partially revived by Queen Mary in 1555, when a Community of men was reorganised in London, at the Priory of St. Bartholomew in Smithfield, and the Sisters were restored to Dartford. In 1559 Elizabeth suppressed the Community of Smithfield, and the same year the Sisters of Dartford were exiled. In 1566 the Dominican Province of England became desolated.*

Although the Province was thus laid waste, it was never entirely extinguished. From time to time Englishmen entered foreign Convents, and a few returned into their native country to labour in the vineyard of Christ. Ambassadors, too, had sometimes foreign Dominicans in their household. The Master-General in 1622 re-

* *Obituary Notices of the Friars Preachers of the English Province.* By Rev. C. F. Raymund Palmer, O.P. (London: Burns & Oates.)

organised the few Dominicans in the country as a Congregation, and appointed a Vicar-General over them. F. Philip Thomas Howard restored monastic discipline, establishing in 1658 a Convent of English Dominicans at Bornhem, in Flanders, and in 1660 a house of Sisters of the Second Order at Vilvorde. Bornhem poured into England a full measure of apostolical missioners, who planted important missions and stations up and down the country, till the French Revolution drove them out of their Belgian house. Since that time, however, their labours have been continued from new foundations.

HINCKLEY, Leicestershire, Priory and Church of St. Peter. A Novitiate was established here in 1814, and a secular school in 1825.

LEICESTER, Priory of Holy Cross, Church of St. Patrick. Holy Cross Priory, the chief house of the Dominicans in the Midlands, though only established some seventy years ago on its present site, yet revives and represents a foundation of very ancient date. As far back as 1247, only thirty years after the birth of the Order itself, and twenty-six years from the death of St. Dominic, the Dominicans had founded in Leicester a Priory under the title of St. Clement, Pope and Martyr. In May 1817 the present Priory was commenced.

In 1882 Holy Cross was formally constituted a "Priory." Besides Holy Cross Church, there is another belonging to the Dominicans, St. Patrick's, in the lower quarter of the town.

LONDON, Haverstock Hill, N.W., Priory of St. Dominic, Southampton Road, Maitland Park Road, opened Oct. 10th, 1867. Church of the Holy Name, opened May 31st, 1883.

NEWCASTLE-ON-TYNE, Northumberland, Priory of St. Dominic (1873), Redbarns; St. Lawrence (1877), Byker (served from St. Dominic's).

PRUDHOE HALL, Prudoe-on-Tyne, Northumberland, Church of Our Lady and St. Cuthbert (1870).

STROUD, Gloucestershire, Church of the Immaculate Conception (1857).

WOODCHESTER, Stroud, Gloucestershire, Priory and Church of the Annunciation (1847-9).

The houses belonging to the Irish Province are:

ATHENRY, Co. Galway, Priory of St. Peter and St. Paul, founded 1241.

ATHY, Co. Kildare, Priory of St. Dominic, founded 1253.

CORK, Priory, St. Mary's of the Isle, Pope's Quay, founded 1229.

DROGHEDA, Co. Louth, Priory of St. Mary Magdalen, founded 1229.

DUBLIN, The Most Holy Saviour (1224); Church, Lower Dominick Street; Convent, 30 Rutland Square.

DUNDALK, Co. Louth, Priory of St. Malachy, founded 1305.

GALWAY, Priory of Our Lady of the Assumption, founded 1488.

KILKENNY, Priory of the Most Holy Trinity, known also as Black Abbey, founded 1225.

LIMERICK, Priory of St. Saviour, founded 1227.

NEWBRIDGE, Co. Kildare, St. Eustace and Companions, and College of St. Thomas, founded at Naas in 1356.

NEWRY, Co. Down, Sacred Heart and St. Catherine of Sienna, founded 1866.

PORTUMNA, Boula, Co. Galway, Priory of St. Peter and St. Paul.

SLIGO, The Holy Cross, founded 1252.

TALLAGHT, Co. Dublin, Our Lady of the Rosary, founded 1855.

TRALEE, Co. Kerry, Holy Cross, founded 1243; restored 1858.

WATERFORD, The Most Holy Saviour, founded 1226.

To the Irish Province also belong the Priories of SS. Sixtus and Clement at Rome, founded 1667, and Our Lady of the Rosary at Lisbon, founded in 1615.

Franciscans or Friars Minor.

Founded by St. Francis of Assisi in 1209. In 1210 Pope Innocent III. verbally approved of the Rule, which was solemnly ratified by Pope Honorius III. in 1223. Crowds of persons, both male and female, desiring to live under his Rule, he founded a Second Order for Nuns, called the Poor Ladies, afterwards Poor Clares, from St. Clare, the first Abbess; and finally a Third or Tertiary Order for persons living in the world. These Tertiaries, in many instances, formed themselves into regular Communities, and still exist, side by side with those lay persons for whom the Third Order was primarily intended. After the death of St. Francis the Order was divided into two great branches, Conventuals and Observantines, and of these there are several subdivisions, two of the most important being the Recollects and Capuchins. The Superior of any Franciscan Monastery is called a Guardian (Custos), and each division is under a Minister-General of its own. As early as 1219 St. Francis sent Brother Angelo of Pisa to England with eight other Friars. These landed at Dover in 1220, and founded their first Convent at Canterbury, and another in Farringdon Within, now known as Christ's Hospital or Blue Coat School. At the dissolution there were sixty-five houses in England.

Habit.—A coarse gray gown, with a pointed hood or capuce attached to it, one under tunic and drawers, and a cord round the waist.

Franciscan Friars Minor (Observance).

CLEVEDON, Somersetshire, Friary and Church of the Immaculate Conception. Founded in 1882 by exiled French Fathers.

SALTASH, Cornwall, Friary and Church of St. Mary of the Angels, founded in 1884. The Religious of this house belong to the French Province of St. Lewis, Bishop, O.S.F., and depend upon the same Superior Provincial as their brethren established in Clevedon, Somersetshire.

ATHLONE. Founded in the thirteenth century. The present Convent was erected in 1870. In 1884 the old church was taken down and rebuilt.

CARRICK-ON-SUIR, Co. Tipperary, Convent, Carrickbeg.

CLONMEL, Co. Tipperary. Founded in 1249.

CORK, Liberty Street.

DROGHEDA. Founded in 1240 by the Plunkets.

DUBLIN, Convent and Church of Adam and Eve, Merchant's Quay.

ENNIS, Co. Clare. Founded 1240.

GALWAY.

KILLARNEY, Co. Kerry. Founded at Irrelagh early in the fifteenth century.

LIMERICK.

MULTYFARNHAM. Founded in 1236.

THURLES, Co. Tipperary.

WATERFORD, Convent, St. Francis Place.

WEXFORD. Founded in the eleventh century.

Franciscan Recollect Fathers.

A branch of the Franciscan Friars of the Observance. Founded by B. John de Puebla 1489. These Friars soon became a separate Congregation. This branch of the Franciscan Order occupies the Convent at Jerusalem, where reside the guardians of the Church of the Holy Sepulchre. They were suppressed in France at the Revolution, but reappeared some years ago at Amiens and other places. In England their houses are:

GLASGOW, Cumberland Street South, Church of St. Francis.

LONDON, The Friary, Stratford, E.; Church of St. Francis Assisi (1770, 1868), Grove Crescent Road, Stratford; Church of St. Anthony of Padua, Forest Gate, Upton, E.; The Elms, Upton Lane, Stratford, E. (French Community).

MANCHESTER, Church of St. Francis of Assisi (1863, 1872), West Gorton.*

Foreign Missions.

HENDON, Middlesex. St. Joseph's Foreign Missionary College of the Sacred Heart, Mill Hill, N.W., was founded by the Bishop of Salford in 1866. The priests who are educated at this College become members of a society of secular priests for the purpose of evangelising the heathen beyond Europe. The society admits also lay Brothers.

LIVERPOOL. St. Peter's School for Foreign Missions at Freshfield, near Liverpool, admits candidates who are not less than sixteen nor more than twenty years of age, to be prepared for Mill Hill, if they have a real desire to devote themselves to the foreign missions in preference to the home missions, and are well recommended by a priest.

Holy Cross (Canons Regular of the).

These Canons, who form a branch of the Augustinian Canons, were restored and reformed

---

* *New Life of St. Francis of Assisi.* By Léopold de Chérancé. (London: Burns & Oates.) *Life of St. Francis of Assisi.* By R. F. O'Connor. (London: Burns & Oates.) *St. Francis and the Franciscans.* (London: Richardson & Son.)

by the Ven. Théodore de Celles (Cellesius) during the pontificate of Innocent III. in 1211. Approved by Innocent III. on the 3rd May 1216, and enriched with many privileges by various Sovereign Pontiffs. They follow the Rule of St. Augustine, with special constitutions of their own.

Their object is the recitation in choir of the Divine Office, combined with the missionary life of a secular priest.

Habit.—White cloth, over which they wear a black scapular, on front of which is a Maltese cross in white and red. They have a black sash round their waist, so that a large black cross is formed in front and behind, on the white ground of the habit; the sash has the form of the Greek cross (letter T); and they wear the canonical cape in black cloth.

One of the special privileges of these Canons is the blessing of beads, by which they attach an Indulgence of five hundred days to each bead.

NEWMARKET, Cambridgeshire, Church of Our Lady Immaculate and St. Etheldreda, founded 1876.

Holy Ghost and the Immaculate Heart of Mary (Congregation of).

This Congregation arose out of the fusion into one, in 1848, of two Institutes—the Congregation of the Holy Ghost and the Missioners of the Immaculate Heart of Mary. The Society is governed by a Superior-General elected for life. Its missions are directed by Bishops or Vicars-Apostolic chosen from its own body. All the members take the three simple vows of religion, at first temporary, afterwards perpetual, and a fourth promise of perseverance in the Congregatiom. Besides the professed members there are the Oblates, who from the age of fourteen, for at least six months, are received into the Congregation as its children, are clothed in the habit, and take the engagement to persevere till their profession. The novitiate is ordinarily for two years. The Congregation always pursues as its main object, after the perfection of its members, the evangelisation of the blacks, especially the blacks of Africa itself. To encourage vocations, the Congregation founds houses primarily devoted to different objects. It has a French Seminary in Rome, canonically erected in 1853, and also two Colleges for secondary education in Ireland. In 1884 the Congregation had eighty houses in different parts of the world.

  BLACKROCK, Co. Dublin. French College.

· CAHIR, Co. Tipperary, Rockwell College, noted for the success of its pupils at the Intermediate Examinations.

Jesuit Fathers (Fathers of the Society of Jesus).

Founded by St. Ignatius of Loyola* at the time of the Reformation, at the Chapel of St. Mary, Montmartre, Paris, 16th August 1534. Approved by Paul III., 27th September 1540, under the title of Clerks Regular of the Society of Jesus, and again by the same Pontiff in 1543, and by Julius III. in 1550. The first establishment was at Rome, where the General of the Order usually resides. Illustrious for the services they have rendered to the Church, and the persecutions and vicissitudes they have endured throughout the world, in propagation and defence of the faith and the spread of education. Jesuits are engaged in the work of foreign missions.

In 1598 there were eighteen Jesuits at work in England, of whom four were in prison. The English Vice-Province was erected in 1619, and the Province in 1623, under Fr. Richard Blount as first Provincial. Fifty-seven of the Order are known to have been martyred in England during the persecutions, concerning some of whom a process of canonisation is pending at Rome.

Rule.—Active and contemplative, mission-

---

* Genelli's *Life of St. Ignatius* (London, 1871); *The Jesuits: their Foundation and History* (London, 1879); *The Catholic Dictionary*, art. "Jesuits"; F. Ravignan, *Life and Institute of the Jesuits.*

JESUIT FATHERS.

ary and educational; renunciation of ecclesiastical dignities; especial obligations of obedience to the Pope and of going on the foreign missions.

Habit.—Ordinary ecclesiastical dress of the country.

Houses, Churches, and Colleges in Great Britain and Ireland are:

ACCRINGTON, Lancashire, Church of the Sacred Heart (1851).

BEDFORD LEIGH, Manchester, Church of St. Joseph (1778-1855).

BLACKPOOL, Lancashire, Church of Sacred Hearts of Jesus and Mary (1854-1857).

BOURNEMOUTH, Hants (Richmond Hill), Oratory of the Sacred Heart (1869).

BRISTOL, Church of St. Mary (1843), on the Quay.

BROUGHTON HALL, Skipton, Yorkshire, Church of the Sacred Heart (1757).

BURY ST. EDMUNDS, Suffolk, 22 Westgate Street, Church of St. Edmund.

CANTERBURY, Hales Place, College of St. Mary (French Fathers).

CHESTERFIELD, Derbyshire, Church of the Annunciation (1853-4); Mount St. Mary's College, for boys, and Church of the Immaculate Conception (1844-46).

CLITHEROE, Lancashire, Church of SS. Michael and John the Evangelist (1847-50).

DALKEITH, N.B., Church of St. David.

DITTON HALL, Widness, Lancashire, Church of St. Michael.

THEOLOGICAL COLLEGE, Ditton, for German Province of Society of Jesus.

EDINBURGH, Lauriston Street, Church of the Sacred Heart of Jesus.

GALASHIELS, Selkirkshire, Church of Our Lady and St. Andrew.

GILLMOSS, Liverpool, Church of St. Swithin (1757-1820).

GLASGOW, Church and College of St. Aloysius, Garnet Hill; Church of St. Joseph, North Woodside Road.

HASTINGS, Sussex, College of St. Stanislaus (French Fathers).

HOLYWELL, Co. Flint, Church of St. Winefride (1833): daily Plenary Indulgence.

JERSEY, St. Helier's, St. Aloysius' House (French Fathers).

LITTLEHAMPTON, Sussex, Apostolic College of St. Joseph (French Fathers).

LIVERPOOL, Salisbury Street, E., Church of St. Francis Xavier; College of St. Francis Xavier (1845-1849).

LONDON, 31 Farm Street, Berkeley Square, W., where the Provincial resides; Church of the Immaculate Conception (1844-5); 12 Earl Street, S.W., Church of St. Mary (1813), Horseferry Road.

LULWORTH CASTLE, Wareham, Dorset, Church of St. Mary (1790).

MANCHESTER, Oxford Road, Church of the Holy Name.

MOLD, Flint, College of St. David (French Fathers); House of Studies for the members of the Province of Lyons (France) of the Society of Jesus. The course of studies comprises classics, with rhetoric, philosophy, and theology (1886).

Besides some Catechisms in the neighbourhood, the mission of Ruthin and the gaol in the same town are attended by some of the Fathers of St. David's College.

OLD WINDSOR, Berks, Beaumont College (St. Stanislaus). In 1854 this property was purchased by the Society of Jesus to serve as the Noviceship of the Order in England. The Novices were not long afterwards transferred to Manresa House, Rohampton, and in October 1861, Beaumont Lodge was opened as a College. At present there are about 180 pupils in residence, but increased accommodation is now being provided for younger boys by the erection of a new junior school, about a quarter of a mile distant from the old house, which will be completed in the course of the year 1887. The

College is conveniently adapted for its purpose, and there is a fine chapel, recently enlarged, to which the Catholics of the neighbourhood are admitted. The library is rich in early English Catholic literature, but is not otherwise very extensive. The administrative and teaching staff of the College consists of some twenty-five members of the Society of Jesus, eight or nine of whom are priests. The course of studies is similar to that of the other Jesuit Colleges in England.

OXFORD, St. Giles', Church of St. Aloysius (1875).

PONTEFRACT, Church of St. Joseph (1800).

PORTICO, near Prescot, Lancashire, Church of Our Lady Help of Christians; House of Tertiaries of the German Province.

PRESCOT, Lancashire, Church of Our Lady Immaculate and St. Joseph (1857).

PRESTON, Lancashire, Church of St. Ignatius (1833-6, enlarged 1858), St. Ignatius Square; Church of St. Mary, Friargate; Church of St. Walburge (1850, 1866), Maudlands; Church of St. Wilfred (1793-1834), Chapel Street.

RHYL, Co. Flint, Church of St. Mary (1863).

RICHMOND, Yorkshire, Church of St. Joseph and St. Francis Xavier (1748-1868).

ROEHAMPTON, S.W., Manresa House, Novitiate and House of Retreat; Church of S. Joseph (1869).

ST. ASAPH, College of St. Beuno. This is an exclusively theological College, being the place where members of the English Province of the Society of Jesus make the studies that immediately prepare them for the priesthood, and where they are ordained. The course ordinarily occupies three or four years. The priesthood is received one year before the end of the course. Church of the Holy Name (1848-49); Church of St. Winefride.

ST. HELENS, Lancashire, Church of St. Mary, Lowe House (1793); Holy Cross (3rd May 1862).

SELKIRK, N.B., Church of Our Lady and St. Joseph.

SKIPTON, Yorks., Church of St. Stephen (1836, 1862).

SLOUGH, Bucks, St. Joseph's House (French Fathers).

STONYHURST COLLEGE, near Blackburn. In 1582 Father Persons, S.J., established a school for English boys at Eu in Normandy, and in 1588 the school seems to have been transplanted to St. Omers, where, in 1592, a new establishment was commenced under the patronage of King Philip of Spain, and here the history of Stonyhurst properly begins. The commencement was small, the number of scholars being limited by the magistrates to fifteen. It soon, however, grew, and during more than a century and a half was much frequented by the Catholic youth of England.

In 1762 the Parliament of Paris determined to expel the Jesuit Fathers from this as from their other establishments, but wished to retain the boys, and put them in charge of other teachers; but the College authorities anticipated the blow by decamping with all their pupils, whom they got across the Flemish frontier, and conducted to Bruges, where they reëstablished their College, and carried it on for eleven years.

In 1773 Pope Clement XIV. suppressed the Society of Jesus, and the Austrian Government accordingly arrested all the Fathers of the College, and it was again proposed to confide the boys to the tuition of State-appointed guardians; but some of the pupils escaped to Liége, where the school flourished till, in 1794, the approach of the French Revolutionary Army, with orders to treat all Englishmen as enemies, enforced another migration. The Continent had ceased to be safe for such an establishment, but England had at last become so; and as Mr. Thomas Weld, an old pupil of Bruges, invited the fugitives to take up their quarters at least for a time at Stonyhurst on his Lancashire property, they betook themselves thither, where they gradually settled down as in a permanent home. The old buildings were little by little adapted or replaced, in accordance with scholastic needs, and within the past decade a large pile has been added, which will, it is hoped, supply all wants for many years to come.

WAKEFIELD, Church of St. Austin (1828).

WARDOUR CASTLE, Tisbury, Wilts, Church of All Saints (1777).

WIGAN, Standish Gate, Church of St. John (1740, 1819).

WORCESTER, Church of St. George, Sansome Place (1685, 1829).

YARMOUTH, GREAT, Church of St. Mary, Regent Road, (1850).

CLANE, Kildare, Clonglowes Wood College.

DROMORE, Co. Down, Novitiate, Loyola House.

DUBLIN, University College, St. Stephen's Green; Church of St. Francis Xavier and residence of Provincial, Upper Gardiner Street; Belvedere College (day-school); House of Retreat, Milltown Park; St. Xavier's College, Great Denmark Street.

GALWAY, College, Belvedere House.

LIMERICK, Church and College (day-school;

College of the Sacred Heart, Mungret, built on the site of the old Abbey of same name.

TULLAMORE, St. Stanislaus' College.

Marist Fathers.

Founded early in the present century, by the Very Rev. Father Colin.

Rule.—Sanctioned by Pius IX. on the 28th February 1873. Prescribes that the members of the Society of Mary unite the active with the contemplative life, working under the protection of the Mother of God. Their works are the training of youth in colleges and ecclesiastical seminaries, the home and foreign missions, and preaching, with other functions of the sacred ministry, in their places of residence.

After twelve or eighteen months' novitiate the candidate makes the three simple and perpetual vows of poverty, chastity, and obedience; but the vow of poverty does not deprive the subject of the right to *possess*, but merely of the free and independent *use* of property. Ten years after their entrance, and when not less than thirty-three years of age, the Marist Fathers go through a second novitiate, and make the vow of stability in the Congregation. There are lay Brothers to fulfil the household duties.

The Society is governed by a Superior-General, elected for life, aided by a Council of four assistants, appointed by the General Chapter, which assembles regularly every seven years.

LONDON, Church of St. Anne (1855), Underwood Street, Mile End New Town; Church of Notre Dame de France (1865-8), Leicester Place, Leicester Square, W.C.; Mission for French and French-speaking people, served by the Marist Fathers, with day-schools for boys, girls, and infants; a hospital and dispensary for foreigners; sermons and confessions in French.

PAIGNTON(Devonshire), Novitiate (St. Mary's Hill), Church of St. Mary.

Founded October 1881, by exiled French Marists. The church and Monastery are fine specimens of ecclesiastical art. The church has been dedicated to the Immaculate Conception. It is the principal novitiate of the Society. The missions intrusted to the Society are numerous and widespread, embracing the English-speaking missions in England, Ireland, America, New Zealand, New Caledonia, and most of the Oceanic Islands. To supply these vastly-extended missions the house at Paignton has been intended as a nursery.

BRIXHAM is also served by the Fathers.

DUBLIN, Scholasticate, Catholic University School (1867), 89 Lower Leeson Street.

DUNDALK, St. Mary's College (1861), Novitiate of the Marist Fathers. Established, with permission of the Holy See, in August 1863.

The Fathers opened a grammar-school in 1861. This was the first Irish establishment of the Marist Fathers. Though the Dundalk house, now St. Mary's College, is still a novitiate, most of the aspirants are sent for their probation to Paignton.

Mission, Congregation of the (also called Lazarists and Vincentian Fathers).

Founded in 1624 by St. Vincent de Paul. Approved by Urban VIII. in 1632, and confirmed by Alexander VII. in 1655. St. Vincent was canonised in 1737, and has recently been declared by Leo XIII. Patron of the Charities of the Universal Church.

The object of this Congregation, besides the personal sanctification of the members, is twofold: the service of the poor and the sanctification of the clergy. The principal means which they employ for the first end are the exercises commonly called "Missions." In addition to these labours of the pulpit and the confessional they instruct the children in the Catechism, visit the sick, reconcile those at variance, and establish religious Confraternities. Missions in different localities occupy eight months of the year. Their services are gratuitous. The sanctification of the clergy is the second object of the Institute, chiefly by taking charge of ecclesiastical seminaries. St. Vincent, after M. Olier, was the principal instrument of Providence in raising up establish-

CONGREGATION OF THE MISSION. 69

ments of this nature, wherein young men could be carefully trained for the duties of the priesthood.* His children have carried on the work ever since. Both in their own houses and throughout the dioceses they frequently conduct spiritual exercises for the clergy and prepare candidates for the immediate reception of Holy Orders. If they adopt any other works, it is only when these works are subservient to the above objects.

Their Rule is an admirable compendium of the Gospel maxims reduced to the practice of daily life. St. Vincent spent over thirty years in its compilation. Each page is stamped with the wisdom, zeal, and charity of the founder. A Pope has said that the perfect practice of it would be sufficient title to canonisation without the proof of miracles. Their vows are poverty, chastity, and obedience, with a fourth vow to persevere in the labours of the Institute.

This Congregation is at present numerous and very widely spread in all parts of the world. Its central house is in Paris, where the Father-General resides.

The Province for the United Kingdom is called the Irish Province, and the houses are:

LANARK, N.B., Church of St. Mary, founded by the late Robert Monteith of Carstairs.

* *Life of St. Vincent de Paul.* By Henry Bedford. (London: Burns & Oates.)

SHEFFIELD, Church of St. Vincent de Paul (1853), Solly Street.

ARMAGH, College of St. Patrick.

BLACKROCK, Dublin, St. Joseph's Novitiate and House of Studies.

CASTLEKNOCK, Dublin, College of St. Vincent.

CORK, Church of St. Vincent.

DRUMCONDRA, Dublin, St. Patrick's Training School for Teachers in National Schools.

DUBLIN, Church of St. Peter, Cabra Road, North Circular Road, Phibsborough.

PARIS, Irish College.

Missionaries of the Sacred Heart of Jesus.

Founded at Issoudun, the very day of the proclamation of the dogma of the Immaculate Conception, Dec. 8th, 1854, by the Abbé Jules Chevalier, Canon, Archpriest of Issoudun, and approved by Pius IX. and Leo XIII.

End.—To propagate in every way devotion to the Sacred Heart of Jesus, to our Lady of the Sacred Heart, and to St. Joseph, friend of the Sacred Heart, that all members of families may accomplish their religious duties.

The last two devotions were founded by the Missionaries of the Sacred Heart, and approved by Pius IX. and Leo XIII.

The Society devotes itself to the apostolic

ministry in various forms, even amongst infidels, and especially those of New Guinea.

It assists the secular clergy and the laity in the work of their personal sanctification, and the propagation of devotion to the Sacred Heart of Jesus. It directs the *petite œuvre* (lesser work) or Apostolic School for the education of poor children who desire to become priests or religious. It accepts the direction of colleges, great and little seminaries, and also parishes, but in this last case with the leave of the Holy See, and without detriment to their rules and customs.

The Mother House of the Society with the Apostolic School is at Issoudun.

Rule.—Nearly the same, but less strict than that of the Society of Jesus.

Habit.—Roman collar, cassock and cloak, a woollen cord knotted, an image of the Sacred Heart on the left side of the cassock, with the motto "May the Sacred Heart of Jesus be everywhere loved."

MADELEY, Shropshire. Founded by the Very Rev. Father Chevalier, founder and first Superior-General of the Society.

Oblate Fathers of St. Charles.

Founded by St. Charles Borromeo in 1578 as a Congregation of secular priests, who "offer" themselves (hence the name) to the Bishop, to be employed by him in any part of the diocese and upon any work he may choose. Introduced into England in 1856 by Dr. (now Cardinal) Manning, with the approbation of Cardinal Wiseman, who obtained for this work a rescript of the Holy See, imparting the apostolical benediction.

LONDON, Church of St. Mary of the Angels (1857), Westmoreland Road, Bayswater, W. (to which are attached the Archconfraternity of the Servants of the Holy Ghost, erected by Leo XIII. 6th April 1879, and the Third Order of St. Francis); Church of Our Lady of the Holy Souls (1872), Bosworth Road, Kensal New Town, W.; Church of St. Francis of Assisi (1860), Portland Place, Portland Road, Notting Hill, W.; College of St. Charles, St. Charles' Square, Ladbroke Grove Road, W. (founded in 1863, and moved to the new buildings, with extensive playgrounds, in 1874); Church of St. Peter and St. Edward (1857-8), Palace Street, Buckingham Gate, S.W.

Oblate Fathers of Mary Immaculate.

Founded by the Rev. Charles Joseph Eugène de Mazenod in 1816. The members of the new Society were at first called Missionaries of Provence; the name they now bear was given to them by Pope Leo XII. in 1826, when he formally approved of the rules and constitutions of the Congregation.

In the interior life and organisation of the

Society the founder wished the government to be thoroughly paternal, and the spirit pervading all its members to be that of the greatest charity. All the Religious bind themselves by vow to the observance of poverty, chastity, and obedience, and to perseverance in the Society.

The Rule insists upon all the discipline, observances, and spiritual exercises compatible with the ministry and works to which the members of the Society devote themselves.

The Congregation is under the government of a Superior-General and four assistants. The field of its labours is divided into Provinces and Vicariates, these being presided over respectively by Provincials and Vicars-Apostolic. Every house has its own Superior. A General Chapter of the Congregation is held every six years.

The Oblate Fathers commenced their labours in England about forty-five years ago. They have devoted themselves chiefly to priestly work among the poor in our large towns, and to preaching missions and retreats in parishes and convents.

The Oblates have many houses in France. Their chief Scholasticate is at Belcamp Hall, Raheny, Co. Dublin; another is in Rome. There is also a flourishing Scholasticate in Canada, and one in Ceylon.*

* *Life of Mgr. de Mazenod.* By the Rev. Robert Cooke, O.M.I. (London: Burns & Oates.)

JERSEY, St. Heliers, St. Thomas, New Street. Founded during the French Revolution, 1793, and placed under the care of the Oblates of Mary Immaculate in November 1880; Church of Our Lady and Holy Martyrs of Japan (1863); Church of St. Matthew (1882); Church of St. Martin (in September 1884 the Oblates took charge of this mission); Apostolic College, The Limes, Green Street (this school was opened after the expulsion from their houses in France).

KILBURN, London, N.W., New Priory, Quex Road; Church of Sacred Heart of Jesus, Quex Road.

When the Oblate Fathers received their welcome to London from his Eminence Cardinal Wiseman in July 1864, Kilburn and Tower Hill were fixed as the new fields for their missionary labour. The first Mass was said in Kilburn on February 2nd, 1865, and in Tower Hill on March 25th of the same year.

The Fathers at first carried on their work in a private house until September 8th, 1868, when their temporary church was opened. The present church, designed by Messrs. Pugin, was opened on May 8th, 1879; it is only part of the large church which it is intended to build. It is dedicated to the Sacred Heart of Jesus.

The Juniorate at Kilburn was opened on January 25th, 1876. Here youths and young men, who are aspirants of the Congregation,

MARY IMMACULATE.

receive their classical education preparatory to their reception into the Novitiate.

LEEDS, Church of St. Mary (1851-66).

LEITH, N.B., 116 Constitution Street; Church of Our Lady Star of the Sea.

LIVERPOOL, Great Crosshall Street, N., Church of the Holy Cross, Great Crosshall Street.

LONDON, 23 Great Prescot Street, Tower Hill, E.; Church of the English Martyrs (new church, 1876), Great Prescot Street.

ROCK FERRY, Birkenhead, Church of St. Anne. Attend the Clarence Reformatory ship.

SICKLINGHALL, Lys Marie, Wetherby, Yorks; Church of the Immaculate Conception (1852). Founded by Peter Middelton, Esq., and offered by him to the O.M.I., who, with the sanction of the Bishop and of their founder, accepted the care of it in 1852.

The house is open to any of the clergy for spiritual retreats, and also to lay gentlemen.

WETHERBY, Church of St. Joseph (1882). Served from Sicklinghall.

GLENCREE, Co. Wicklow (1860), Reformatory of St. Kevin (office, 16 William Street, Dublin). This Reformatory School was established and opened in 1859, and has been in charge of the Oblates of Mary Immaculate since. In addition to the members of the Community there are some competent tradesmen employed to instruct the boys in the different departments. About two hundred boys are learning trades, and the remainder are employed on the farm.

INCHICORE, Dublin, House of Retreat.

RAHENY, Dublin, Belcamp Hall, Scholasticate. Exiled French Fathers from Burgundy, where there were a large number of scholastics belonging to the Order.

The Community is entirely composed of members of the Order, and generally numbers about fifty students and professors.

The course of studies embraces the various branches of an ecclesiastical education.

When the students are ordained priests, they are sent to the missions belonging to the Order in Europe, America, Asia, and Africa.

STILLORGAN, Co. Dublin, Lourdes House Novitiate. It was formerly at Glenmary, Co. Wicklow; but as the house there proved too small for the requirements of the Community, a more suitable residence was sought for and acquired on October 10th, 1863. The Novitiate House received the name of "Lourdes House" in January 1886, as a token of gratitude to our Lady of Lourdes. To this house are transferred the juniors of the Congregation, when they have finished their course of classical studies in the Juniorate at Kilburn. The novices are divided into two classes—scholastic novices intending to become Oblate Fathers, and other novices wishing to be Oblate lay Brothers. The noviceship lasts for one year, at the end of which term the novices make their vows for one year. The scholastic novices are then sent, according to the decision of their Superiors, either to the Scholasticate at Raheny (Co. Dublin), or to that in Rome, where, at the expiration of a year, they make their profession for life. The other novices receive their obedience for one of the houses of the Province.

Oratorians, or Fathers of the Oratory.

A Congregation of secular priests founded in 1575 by St. Philip Neri,* who received the name of Oratorians from their Oratory or Chapel of St. Girolamo, and their practice of daily summoning the people to prayer. The Community was approved by Gregory XIII., 21st July 1575, who bestowed upon St. Philip the Church of Santa Maria in Vallicella. Constitutions confirmed by Paul V., 21st February 1612.

Rule.—No vows; prayer, daily preaching, and administration of the Sacraments.

Habit.—Ordinary ecclesiastic, with open collar.

Introduced into England by Dr. (now Cardinal) Newman in 1847—first at Mary Vale;

* *Life of St. Philip Neri.* By the Rev. T. A. Pope. (London: Burns & Oates.) *The Excellences of the Congregation of the Oratory of St. Philip Neri.* By the Rev. F. J. Antrobus. (London: Burns & Oates.)

then St. Wilfrid's, Staffordshire; and finally, in 1849, at Birmingham. The same year a branch was sent to London under the Rev. Frederick William Faber (who died 26th September 1863), establishing themselves first in King William Street, Strand. In 1854 they removed to Brompton, where they have built one of the finest Catholic churches in the kingdom.

BIRMINGHAM, Church of the Immaculate Conception (1849), Hagley Road (his Eminence Cardinal Newman Superior); Brothers of the Little Oratory; the Oratory School; Orphanage of St. Philip Neri, Oliver Road, Lady Wood.

LONDON, Church of the Immaculate Heart of Mary (new church consecrated 16th April 1884), Brompton Road, South Kensington, S.W. (opened in King William Street, Strand, 1849; removed to South Kensington 1854); Brotherhood of the Little Oratory.

The Fathers attend the parish attached to their church, with four hospitals and other charitable institutions.

Passionist Fathers.

Their full title is "Congregation of the Discalced Clerks of the Most Holy Cross and Passion of our Lord Jesus Christ," and they were founded in 1720 by St. Paul of the Cross. Approved by Benedict XIV. in 1741, and confirmed 1746; also by Clement XIV. in 1769 and Pius VI. in 1785. Clement XIV. bestowed on the Community the Church of SS. Giovanni e Paolo on the Cœlian Hill. The Rule is very austere. They fast three days in every week besides Advent and Lent, wear sandals, rise at night, and recite in choir the canonical hours. They divide their time between contemplation and action, being indefatigable in giving missions and retreats, &c. A General Chapter is held every six years for the election of a new Father-General and other officers. Provincial Chapters for the election of new Provincials and new Rectors are held once in three years.

The object of the Congregation is the sanctification of its own members and the salvation of others. They take simple vows of poverty, chastity, and obedience, and a fourth one to promote devotion to the Passion of our Lord. On the day of their profession they make a vow of perseverance in the Congregation.

Habit.—Black, with badge of the Passion in white letters on the breast, and mantle. Discalced.* Although to work for the conversion of England was one of the most ardent wishes of St. Paul of the Cross, his sons did not come to these countries till 1842, the first to arrive being Father Dominic of the Mother of God, who received Dr. (now Cardinal) Newman into the Church. The Hon. George Spencer, so well known and revered as Father Ignatius,

* *Life of St. Paul of the Cross.* (London.) *Life of Father Ignatius.* (Spencer, London.)

was one of the first who entered the Novitiate of the Passionists in England.

The houses of the Anglo-Hibernian Province are:

BROADWAY, Worcestershire, St. Saviour's Retreat, previously at Woodchester, St. Wilfrid's, Cotton, Hull, and Aston, Stone.

GLASGOW, N.B., Church of St. Mungo, Parson Street (1865).

HARBORNE, Birmingham, St. Mary's Retreat (1870).

HIGHGATE, London, Highgate Hill, N., St. Joseph's Retreat, previously at Hampstead and The Hyde, Edgware Road.

SUTTON, St. Helens, Lancashire, St. Anne's Retreat (1850).

BELFAST, Holy Cross, Crumlin Road.

DUBLIN, Retreat of St. Paul of the Cross, Mount Argus, Harold's Cross (1856). Mount Argus the first foundation of the Passionists in Ireland. For architectural beauty joined to rigid monastic simplicity, Mount Argus, if not unequalled, is certainly unsurpassed by any building of its nature in Ireland.

Pious Society of Missions.

This is a Congregation of secular priests living in community, founded by the servant of God, Vincent Pallotti, in 1835, and confirmed by Gregory XVI. The object of the Pious

Society is to revive the Faith among Catholics, and to spread it among heathen nations, to enkindle charity by promoting good works, and to unite both the secular and regular clergy in carrying out the works of the ministry.

The members of this Society, though living in community, are not bound by vows, but promise to live to the end of their lives in poverty, chastity, obedience, and perseverance.

Besides the Congregation of priests living in community, there is attached to it a body of Nuns, who devote themselves to the education of the poor and orphans; and also a body of laics of both sexes, who are called Aggregates, whose duty it is to assist the Society by supplying means, both spiritual and temporal, to carry out the works of the same.

LONDON, St. Peter's Italian Church, Hatton Garden, E.C.

HASTINGS, St. Mary's Star of the Sea.

Premonstratensians.

This celebrated Order of Regular Canons was founded in 1119-20 by St. Norbert. St. Norbert gave his Canons the Rule of St. Augustine, with special constitutions of his own. He imposed on them perpetual fasting and entire abstinence from meat; but in the course of time relaxations crept in which led to several reformations. Introduced into England in 1140.

The five particular ends of the Order are: the praises of God in the choir, zeal for souls, the spirit of penance, devotion to the Blessed Sacrament, devotion to our Lady. This Order did good service to the Church in the Middle Ages, when there were few, if any, regular seminaries for the secular clergy, and when each of the thousand Monasteries of that Order was as a seminary, from which learned and devoted White Canons were sent out to serve the parish churches as parish priests, with great spiritual fruit, as attested by several Popes and Bishops of those times.

The Canons of this Order possess the unique privilege of eligibility to the charge of secular parishes without Papal dispensation.

Habit.—White cassock and rochet, long white cloak and white cap; whence they were called White Canons.

In 1872[*] the Order was brought back to England by T. A. Young, Esq., K.S.G., who founded two cells belonging to the Belgian Province. The General of the Belgian Province is the Abbot of Strahow, Prague, Bohemia, and the Provincial is the Abbot of Tongerloo. The English novices of this Province are sent to the Novitiate at Tongerloo, in Belgium.

CROWLE, Doncaster, Lincolnshire, Church of St. Norbert and the Blessed Sacrament

---

[*] *Life of St. Norbert.* (London: Burns & Oates.)

(1870-2). This church is the centre in England of the Confraternity of the mass of Reparation. The Norbertine Canons of Crowle have the missionary charge of the isle of Axholme. They have also a chapel-of-ease at Luddington, and conduct services at Epworth.

SPALDING, Lincolnshire, Church of the Immaculate Conception and St. Norbert. This Community consists of four Canons, who are residing in temporary buildings.

STORRINGTON, near Pulborough, Sussex, Priory of Our Lady of England; Church of the Holy Trinity; Novitiate of the Premonstratensian Order of the Primitive Observance. The Canons of this Community belong to the Congregation of the Primitive Observance founded at Frigolet. Expelled by the French Government from their Abbey of St. Michael de Frigolet, they have established themselves permanently in England, to the conversion of which they specially devote themselves.

Redemptorist Fathers (Congregation of the Most Holy Redeemer).

Founded in 1732, at Scala, Italy, by St. Alphonsus Liguori. The Congregation was approved by Benedict XIV. on the 25th of February 1749.

Rule.—The members, besides the three simple but perpetual vows of poverty, chastity, and obedience, bind themselves by a vow of perseverance in the Institute. They refuse all benefices, offices, or dignities outside their own Congregation, except by special command and dispensation from the Pope. Their main occupation is the preaching of missions and retreats to all classes of persons, but with a preference for such as are the most neglected, especially in remote country districts.

The Congregation is under the government of a Superior-General, called the Rector-Major, who lives in Rome, is elected for life by a General Chapter, and is assisted by six Consultors. The Provincials and the Rectors of houses are appointed for a term of three years by the Rector-Major, and their term of office may be renewed at his discretion.

CLAPHAM, S.W., House and Church of Our Immaculate Lady of Victories (1849-52), Clapham Park Road.

BISHOP ETON, Wavertree, near Liverpool, Monastery and Church of Our Lady of the Annunciation. The present beautiful church, designed by the younger Pugin, was opened June 15th, 1858. It is dedicated in honour of our Blessed Lady, under the title of her Annunciation. At Bishop Eton is the Novitiate of the English Province of the Redemptorists, which includes also Ireland and Scotland. The Novitiate buildings were added some twenty-five years ago. Those of the clergy and laity who desire to make private retreats can at all times be received for that purpose in the house. A general retreat to gentlemen is given annually during Passion Week.

PERTH, N.B., Church and House of Our Lady of Perpetual Succour, Kinnoull Hill.

TEIGNMOUTH, Co. Devon, Church of St. Joseph (1875-80); House of Studies of the Congregation of the Most Holy Redeemer.

Those of the clergy and laity who desire to make private retreats can at all times be received for that purpose. Applications to be addressed to the Father Rector.

DUNDALK (Convent established Sept. 1876).

LIMERICK, House and Church of the Redemptorist Fathers, Mount St. Alphonsus, Limerick, who came to Limerick in 1853. They bought land in the suburbs of the city, near the river Shannon, and built on it a small brick church.

The foundation-stone of the Convent was laid in 1856, and the foundation-stone of the splendid church was laid in 1858, and dedicated 1862. A tower and spire were added afterwards, both designed by Goldie and Child.

Servite Fathers (Servants of Mary).

Founded in 1233 by seven merchants of Florence, called Monaldi, Manetti, Antella, Amidei, Uguccioni, Sostegni, and Falconieri. The

Order was largely extended by St. Philip Benizi,* who was elected its fifth General in 1274. It was approved by Pope Alexander IV., confirmed by Gregory X. at the General Council of Lyons in 1274, and again approved and confirmed by Benedict XI. in 1304. In 1418 it was ranked amongst the mendicant Orders by Martin V., the privilege being confirmed by Innocent VIII. in 1487. They have a second Order of cloistered Nuns and a Tertiary Order, some of whom are regulars and live in community, and others secular living in the world.

Rule of St. Augustine, with additional constitutions. Special devotion to Our Lady of the Seven Dolours, the Confraternity of which was established by them, and is under their authority.

Habit.—Tunic, scapular, cloak, and hood, all of black serge.

LONDON, St. Mary's Priory, 264 Fulham Road, S.W.; Church of Sacred and Sorrowing Hearts of Jesus and Mary (1867-75), Fulham Road.

BOGNOR, Co. Sussex, Convent, The Priory; Church of Our Lady of Seven Dolours, Clarence Road (founded October 26th, 1881).

* *Life of St. Philip Benizi.* (London: Burns & Oates.)

PART II. BROTHERS.

Alexian or Cellite Brothers.

A religious Congregation devoted to the works of nursing the sick, especially in time of pestilence; lunatic asylums and epileptic patients are under their charge; the laying-out and burying the dead, and the management of cemeteries. Founded in 1325 at Aix-la-Chapelle; formally approved and confirmed in 1377 by a Brief from Pope Gregory XI., also by Eugenius IV., 1431; Nicholas V., Pius II. New privileges were granted by Pope Sixtus IV., 1472; Pope Julius, 1506; Pope Clement XI., 1709; and Pius IX., 1870.

MANCHESTER, St. Mary's Home, Newton Heath, for Epileptic Patients and Nervous Debility, under the patronage of his Lordship Bishop of Salford.

With the Home is connected the English Novitiate, Manchester; St. Joseph's Catholic Cemetery, Moston Lane; St. Joseph's Cemetery, North Ormsby Road, Middlesbrough.

Carmelite (Tertian Brothers).

Communities of laymen living under the

Rule and in connection with the Discalced Carmelite Fathers.

CLONDALKIN, Co. Dublin, Monastery of St. Joseph; superior school.

DRUMCONDRA, Dublin, St. Joseph's Asylum for Male Blind. The pupils are educated according to the Braille system, and, in addition, they are taught music, together with trades of various kinds, which enable many of them in after life, who may choose to leave the Institute, to earn a livelihood.

Charity, Brothers of (Congregation of).

This Brotherhood was established in November 1809 by the Rev. Canon Triest, better known as the St. Vincent de Paul of Belgium. Its parent house is in Ghent, Belgium. The Provincial Branch of Canada was established in Montreal in 1865. The special aim of this Congregation is the sanctification of its own members, who devote themselves to the care of the aged, sick, insane, and incurable men; to the instruction of boys of all and every condition; but, above all, of orphans, abandoned children, deaf and dumb, and blind. The Congregation has at present four Novitiates: one in Belgium, at Ghent; one in Ireland, at Waterford; another in Canada, at Longue Pointe; and one in the United States, at Detroit, Michigan, at the Orphan Asylum of St. Anthony, Gratiat Street.

Young men intending to become members of this religious Congregation must be of goodwill and always ready to perform the duties above-mentioned. None are admitted except with the best references.

BELMONT PARK, Waterford, St. Patrick's Institution for the Insane.

Christian Schools (Brothers of the).

Founded in 1680 at Reims by the Venerable Jean Baptiste de la Salle, a Canon of that town, with the object of promoting the Christian education of youth.* He is regarded as the originator of primary schools and primary instruction, which till his time had been confounded with secondary. The Rule required that the Brothers who bound themselves by vow to devote their lives to teaching in the schools, and wore the religious habit, should be and remain laymen, and this has continued to be the practice of the Congregation ever since. For the training of the Brothers the founder instituted a Novitiate; for that of the professors, &c., a normal school. Founded at Reims in 1685, this was the first *training-school* for primary teachers in Europe.

The Brothers take the three religious vows

* The saintly founder died at Rouen in 1719. He was declared venerable in 1840 by Pope Gregory XVI. A decree attesting that he practised virtue in a heroic degree was promulgated in 1873.

after having attained to at least twenty-three years of age.

Habit.—A long black cassock, with a cloak over it fastened by clasps, a falling collar with two ends, and wide-brimmed hat.

The Bull of approbation was granted by Benedict XIII. in 1725, elevating them into a religious Congregation. This was the only religious institution that survived the suppression of the Orders at the French Revolution, being authorised to reopen its schools immediately after the Concordat of 1801, and acquiring a legal status by the decree of 17th March 1808, establishing the University of France. The Mother House is in Paris, and the Superior-General resides here.

The establishments conducted by the Brothers of the Christian Schools comprise elementary, middle class, art, and agricultural schools; colleges, orphanages, and training-schools for lay teachers. The most suitable age for entering the Institute is from sixteen to twenty-five years. Candidates may, however, be admitted from the age of thirteen to sixteen in the "Preparatory Novitiate," in order to test their vocation and to prepare themselves for the Novitiate proper. The qualities indispensably required in every aspirant admit of the following divisions: (1) Physical: health and strength that will enable him to endure the fatigues of teaching; a gentlemanly appearance, without any apparent deformity; (2) Intellectual: a sound judgment, with abilities either to acquire the necessary instruction, or to exercise some of the ordinary offices in the Community; (3) Moral: a docile and sociable disposition, detachment from worldly goods and interests, zeal for the glory of God, for the salvation of children, and for his own perfection.

LONDON:
Clapham, St. Joseph's College, 49 High Street; St. Mary's Parochial Schools.

Kennington, St. Joseph's Academy, 167 Kennington Lane.

MANCHESTER, Longsight, St. Joseph's Industrial School, Richmond Grove.

CHANNEL ISLANDS, Jersey, St. Helier, St. Thomas's Schools, Berri House.

CASTLETOWN, Queen's County, De la Salle Retreat, Novitiate, Scholasticate; Monastery; National School.

KILDARE, Monastery National School.

Christian Brothers (Irish).

Founded by Mr. Edmond Rice of Waterford. The first schools were opened 1st May 1804. Up to 1816 the Brothers had no distinctive Rule, but followed, as far as circumstances would allow, that of the Presentation Nuns. This being inconvenient, at a general meeting in Waterford in 1817 it was agreed to adopt the Rule of the French Brothers with modifications. These constitutions were formally approved by Pope Pius VII. on the 5th September 1820. The government consists of a Superior-General, elected for life, with two assistants, eight Directors of principal houses, and eight Ancient Brothers. The Head House and Novitiate of the Institute is at Marino, Dublin, where the Superior-General and his assistants reside.

ADARE, Co. Limerick, St. Joseph's. Number of schools, two. Founded and endowed by the Earl of Dunraven in 1854 for the education of the children of his tenantry and of the locality. Number of pupils, 140.

ARMAGH. The Christian Brothers were introduced into this place by the late Cardinal Cullen. St. Patrick's, 2.

ATHY, Co. Kildare, St. John's, 3.

BALLINROBE, Co. Mayo, 2.

BELFAST, St. Mary's (4), 450; St. Patrick's (4), 400; St. Malachy's (2), 150: 10.

BRUFF, Co. Limerick, St. Patrick's, 2.

CAHIRCIVEEN, Co. Kerry, 2.

CALLAN, Co. Kilkenny, St. Ignatius', 2.

CARLOW, St. Mary's, 4.

CARRICK-ON-SUIR, Co. Tipperary, Mount St. Nicholas (2), 200; the Green (2), 200 : 4.

CASHEL, Co. Tipperary (3), 200.

CAVAN, 3.

CHARLEVILLE, Co. Cork, 2.

CLAREN BRIDGE, Co. Galway, 1.

CLONMEL, Co. Tipperary, SS. Peter and Paul (4), 450; St. Mary's, Irishtown (2), 250: 6.

CORK, Our Lady's Mount (12), 1200; Sullivan's Quay (3), 300; Blarney Street (5), 500: 20.

DINGLE, Co. Kerry, 4.

DONERAILE, Co. Cork, 2.

DOON, 2.

DROGHEDA, Co. Louth, St. Joseph s 4), 340; West Gate (2), 150: 6.

DUBLIN :

> ARTANE, Industrial Schools.
> BALDOYLE (Junior Novitiate).
> CABRA (Deaf and Dumb), 1.
> GLASNEVIN (Orphanage), 1.
> MARINO (Novitiate).
> RICHMOND STREET North (6), 800 St. Lawrence O'Toole's, (2), 250; St. Mary's Place (4), 500; Great Strand Street (4), 400: 1950.

JAMES STREET, St. James's (4), 450; Inchicore (2), 100.

SYNGE STREET, St. Kevin's (4), 500; Francis Street (4), 400.

BRUNSWICK STREET North, St. Paul's, 4.

WESTLAND ROW, St. Andrew's, 6.

DUNDALK, Co. Louth, St. Aloysius', 4.

DUNGARVAN, Co. Waterford, 4.

ENNIS, Co. Clare, St. Mary's, 4.

ENNISCORTHY, Co. Wexford, St. Mary's, 3.

ENNISTYMON, Co. Clare, Mount St. Joseph, 2.

FERMOY, Co. Cork, 2.

GALWAY (Industrial School).

GOREY, Co. Wexford, 2.

KELLS, Co. Meath, St. Joseph's.

KILCOCK, Co. Kildare, St. Joseph's, 2.

KILKENNY, St. Mary's, 3.

KILRUSH, Co. Clare, 3.

KINGSTOWN, St. Michael's, Eblana Avenue, 4.

LETTERFRACK, County Galway, Industrial School (1), 75.

LIMERICK, St. Michael's (10), 900; St. John's (2), 250; St. Mary's (4), 350; St. Munchin's (2), 200.

Industrial School (2), 160.

LISMORE, Co. Waterford, 2.

CHRISTIAN BROTHERS.

LONDONDERRY, 4.

MARYBOROUGH, Queen's Co., 2.

MIDLETON, Co. Cork, St. Finbar's, 4.

MITCHELSTOWN, Co. Cork, 3.

MONAGHAN, St. Maccartan's, 2.

MONASTEREVAN, Co. Kildare, 2.

MULLINGAR, Co. Westmeath, St. Mary's.

NAAS, Co. Kildare, St. Patrick's, 2.

NENAGH, Co. Tipperary, St. Joseph's, 4.

NEW ROSS, Co. Wexford, Mount St. Joseph, 2.

NEWRY, Co. Down, Mount St. Joseph (1), 120; St. Peter's (2), 250; Kilmorey Street (2), 200: 5.

OMAGH, Co. Tyrone, Mount St. Columba, 2.

PORTARLINGTON, Queen's Co., 2.

THURLES, Co. Tipperary, 4.

TIPPERARY, 2.

TRALEE, Co. Kerry, St. Mary's, 4.; Industrial School, 1.

TRAMORE, Co. Waterford, St. Oteran's, 2.

TUAM, Co. Galway, St. Patrick's, 3.

TULLAMORE, King's Co., St. Patrick's, 2.

WATERFORD, Mount Sion (10), 900; St. Patrick's (2), 200; St. John's (2), 240: 14.

Westport, Co. Mayo, 3.
Wexford, St. Joseph's, 3.
Selsker, 2.
Youghal, Co. Cork, 4.

Franciscan Brothers.

These Religious follow the Rule of the Third Order of St. Francis of Assisi. Though this Third Order was in the first instance founded for seculars living in the world, yet even during the lifetime of the holy founder Congregations of Religious were formed, both male and female, who followed this Rule as distinct from that of the First and Second Orders. The Irish Province was restored about the beginning of this century, and soon afterwards the Mountbellew Monastery, which is the parent house of the Irish portion of the Third Order, was founded in 1818 in the diocese of Tuam, by some Religious sent for that purpose by the Provincial of the Franciscan Order, under whose jurisdiction they were. But in 1830 this jurisdiction was transferred to the Ordinary of the diocese *pro tem.* by Pope Pius VIII., and since then Mountbellew Monastery and its many filiations in this country and America have remained under the jurisdiction of the Bishops, but by Papal sanction and with full right to all the privileges of the Order.

Habit.—Brown, of the same shape as that

worn by members of the First Order. The most suitable age for admission to this Order is between seventeen and twenty-five.

ACHILL, Island of. Founded in 1852 from Roundstone, Co. Galway.

ANNADOWN. Founded in 1850 by Brother Elias Silk, from Errew Monastery, on a site given by the late Francis Blake, Esq., J.P., of Cregg Castle. The Monastery is at present being enlarged and undergoing alterations to make it suitable for a Novitiate for the Order, which was established here in the year 1884.

BROOKLODGE.

CLARA, King's Co. Founded on the 25th August 1821 by Brother Lewis Matthew Delahunt, who gave his own house and lands for its foundation and maintenance.

CLIFDEN.

CUMMER.

ERREW.

FARAGHER. Founded about the year 1856 from Clara.

KILKERRIN.

KILTULLAGH, Ballinlough, Co. Roscommon, St. Joseph's Franciscan Monastery and Schools.

MOUNT BELLEW (Portiuncula Monastery and Academy of St. Francis), Boarding School for students intended for the higher Colleges

H

and Universities as well as for the Civil Service. (Established 1820.)

PARTRY.

ROUNDSTONE, Co. Galway. Founded 1835.

Hospitallers, Brothers (of St. John of God).

The Order of Brothers Hospitallers of St. John of God, known too as "Fratres Hospitalitatis," "Fate bene Fratelli," or "Frères de la Charité," was founded in Spain in the sixteenth century, and was approved by Pope St. Pius V. in 1572, by Pope Sixtus V. in 1586, and confirmed by Pope Paul V. in 1617.

The Rule of this Order, based on that of St. Augüstine, was drawn up six years after the death of the founder, but religious vows were only introduced into it in 1570.

The Brothers Hospitallers seek, with their own sanctification, their neighbours' spiritual and temporal welfare, but chiefly the good of the sick, infirm, and poor. To the three solemn vows of religion they add a fourth, of serving the sick and poor for life.

The Order is governed by a Prior-General who resides in Rome, and is composed of laymen, though priests, desiring to devote their sacred ministry to the brethren and the patients, are received. The members live in Hospital-Convents, under a Prior, where they spend their time in serving the sick, and in performing the usual duties and pious exercises of religious life. The members assist together daily at Holy Mass, prayers, and meditation, the recital of the Office of our Lady, spiritual reading, meals, and recreation.

The houses of the Order are supported by endowments, by yearly grants from governments, corporations, or societies, by voluntary alms and subscriptions, by the pension paid by patients, and by the labour and questing of the brethren.

Young men of good character, sound health, and possessing aptitude for the duties of the Order, who are resolved to serve God generously in practising the virtues of religion, and disposed too to serve the sick and poor for His sake, are admitted as postulants. After a trial of six months, postulants are admitted to the religious habit. No novice is admitted to profession before twelve months' noviceship.

Every aspirant is required:

(a) To produce a certificate from his parish priest attesting good character, as also a certificate of baptism.

(b) To provide an outfit, linen, and underclothing, and a first supply of wearing apparel.

(c) To deposit a sufficient sum of money to defray expenses of return home should he wish to withdraw or be deemed unsuited for the Order.

The Novitiate for the United Kingdom is

at Lyons for the present, until a larger number of houses will admit of the erection of an English Province.

Habit.—A black robe, with a black leather cincture, and long black scapular and hood.

DUBLIN, Stillorgan Castle.

This institution has been established for the care of mentally-afflicted gentlemen.

Stillorgan is situated on an elevation on the south side of the metropolis; it is highly recommended for the purity of its air, and is much resorted to by invalids on account of the combination of the sea and mountain air. Dublin is five miles distant, and can be easily reached by both Stillorgan and Blackrock Railway Station.

This institution offers, with the advantages of home country life, the benefit of attendance by religious men whose special vocation is the care of the sick.

A chapel is attached to the establishment, in which patients may daily receive the consolations of religion.

SCORTON, Catterick, Yorkshire, Hospital of St. John of God.

This benevolent institution has been newly founded for the treatment of infirm and incurable male patients—such cases as are not admitted into the ordinary hospitals.

The salubrious and favourable position,

the purity and invigorating air of the country, the close proximity to a railway-station on a branch of the North-Eastern line, place the institution under the most favourable circumstances for carrying out the objects for which it is intended.

Josephites (Brothers of St. Joseph).

Founded in 1817, by Canon van Crombrugghe, at Grammont, in Belgium, for giving a good education to the sons of the commercial and industrial classes.

WEYBRIDGE, Surrey, College of St. George, Woburn Park, for the teaching of the upper and middle classes.

Marist Brothers (Little Brothers of Mary).

Founded in 1817 at Lavalle, near St. Chamond, in the diocese of Lyons, by the Abbé Champagnat, a Marist Father. Approved by the Holy See in January 1863. Introduced into these countries in 1852, and into the Colonies in 1867. The objects of the Brotherhood are their own sanctification, and the Christian education of youth, in connection with parish schools, middle-class, day, and evening schools, and boarding schools. The Mother House is at St. Genis-Laval, near Lyons. The Novitiate for the British Isles is at Dumfries, Scotland.

Habit.—Black soutane and mantle, with cord, cross, and white rabat.

DUMFRIES, N.B., College of St. Joseph, for classical and commercial education, &c. Novitiate at Mount St. Michael (for training young, men between seventeen and twenty-five, desirous of joining the Order, and of devoting their lives to the Catholic education of youth). The Brothers have also Juniorates at Glasgow, London, and Dundee, for boys between the ages of thirteen and seventeen.

DUNDEE, N.B., Forebank House.

EDINBURGH, N.B., 12 Mayfield, Easter Road.

GLASGOW, N.B., 32 Parson Street and 71 Charlotte Street.

JARROW-ON-TYNE, Durham, Poor Schools.

LONDON: Islington, N.; Maiden Lane, W.C.; 47 Lower Park Road, Peckham, S.E. (Middle Class School); St. Patrick's, Soho, W.; St. Aloysius, 9 Polygon, Clarendon Square, Somers Town, N.W.; 8 Albert Place, Spicer Street, Spitalfields, E. (Parochial and Middle Class Schools).

ATHLONE, Monastery of St. Mary.

Mercy (Our Lady of), Brothers of

This religious Institute was founded by the late Monsignor Canon Scheppers, at Malines, Belgium.

Its chief object is the instruction and Christian education of youth. The favourable testimony received from the Bishops, not only of Belgium, but also of England and the Papal States (to which the Congregation has been extended), and, above all, the recommendation of his Eminence Cardinal Pecci (our present Sovereign Pontiff, Leo XIII.), induced the late Holy Father, Pius IX., to give his approval to the Congregation and to its rules. The late Cardinal Wiseman invited the Brothers of Mercy to the archdiocese of Westminster in 1855.

The Congregation of the Brothers of Mercy has already several English and Irish members. Youths who feel themselves called by God to this religious Institute may obtain all necessary information on application to the Director of St. Aloysius's Boarding School, Highgate, London, or to the Superior-General at Malines, Belgium.

LITTLE ILFORD, Essex.

LONDON: Brook Green, Hammersmith, W.; Highgate, N., Boarding School of St. Aloysius, Belle Vue House, Hornsey Lane.

NORTH HYDE, near Southall, Middlesex, Poor Law School, for boys from the workhouse, over seven years of age, and those chargeable to the parish funds. Present number, 640. Founded 1847.

PLAISTOW, Essex, Reformatory School of St. Edward, Boleyn Castle.

Presentation (Brothers of).

Object, educational.

DARTFORD, Kent, Industrial School of St. Vincent, for boys.

BIRR, King's Co., Monastery of St. Brendan. School opened 2nd October 1878. Pupils, 500.

CORK, Douglas Street, Green Mount, and Lancaster Quay. 2000 pupils.

KILLARNEY, Co. Kerry, schools with 800 pupils, Milltown.

Patricians (St. Patrick, Brothers of).

Object, educational.

FETHARD, Co. Tipperary, Monastery of St. Patrick.

GALWAY. Primary schools, with 1000 pupils.

St. Vincent de Paul (Brothers of).

Founded by M. le Prévost at Paris in 1846. The statutes of the Congregation were formally approved by the Holy See on the 10th May 1869.

This Congregation consists of clerical and lay Brothers. The lay Brothers participate actively with their priestly associates in the work allotted to both on the same footing, and are equally entitled to any office for which the priestly character is not absolutely requisite.

The Congregation cares for the temporal and spiritual wants of the working classes. In furthering the interests of the latter, their labours are portioned out under several distinct departments. The Patronages for Apprentice Boys—each Patronage including a house, with a chapel, class-rooms, play-grounds, and a gymnasium, the latter serving on weekdays for a night school, where the boys receive primary and professional instruction. Besides this there are classes of history for the more advanced. The Working Men's Families; the Directors of Patronages and Clubs make arrangements with respectable married men or widows, to secure board and lodging accommodation for homeless boys and working men. The Christian Workshops, organised by the Directors of Patronages, who seek every opportunity to obtain desirable situations for apprentice-boys wanting employment, visiting them in their factories, giving them their protection, affording religious instruction to youths and adults, assisting the poor, and visiting the workman in his sickness. The Orphanages. The Normal Schools, for the proper training of intending members of the Congregation, comprising under the title of a single institution a seminary for ecclesiastical students, an academy for teachers, and a novitiate for all. The Little Seminary, for the instruction of those who, not having as yet made any classical studies, aspire to attain to the priesthood.

Lurgan.

Xaverian Brothers.

Founded in 1839 by Theodore James Ryken for the Christian education of youth. He began the institution of the Congregation at Bruges, and on the 22nd October 1846 he, with twelve young Brothers, made their profession, taking himself the name of St. Francis Xavier, who was chosen Patron of the Congregation.

In 1848 Brother Francis set out for England, where he planted the first branch of the Congregation. That branch has been steadily growing, and they now conduct several flourishing educational establishments.

The end of the Congregation is the perfection of its own members, and the Christian education of youth.

The age for admitting members is from fifteen to thirty years.

The necessary qualifications are good health, sound constitution, piety without singularity, and a willingness to be instructed so as to become useful members.

The time of probation is two years, the whole or part whereof is to be spent in the Novitiate.

After the expiration of the term of noviceship, they are allowed to take the vows of poverty, chastity, and obedience, provided their behaviour has given entire satisfaction.

LONDON, Hammersmith, W.

MAYFIELD, Hurst Green, Sussex.

MANCHESTER : Catholic Collegiate Institute (Boarding and Day School), 54 Grosvenor Square, Oxford Road; Public Elementary School of St. Augustine.

PRESTON, Lancashire, St. Ingatius' Middle School; Elementary Schools, St. Ignatius' and St. Walburge's.

PART III. WOMEN.

Assumption (Nuns of the).

Founded in 1839, by Monseigneur Affre, Archbishop of Paris, who lost his life from a bullet received while endeavouring to quell the riots of 25th June 1848, in the Faubourg St. Antoine, dying two days afterwards, and Madame Milleret (Marie Eugénie de Jésus), the first Mother-General, for the perpetual adoration of the Blessed Sacrament, and the education of the higher classes. The Mother House is at Auteuil, near Paris.

Rule of St. Augustine. Enclosure.

Habit.—Violet, with white cross on the breast, violet girdle and tassel hanging from waist, and white veil. For church ceremonies white cloak, with purple cross on left shoulder. The professed wear a gold ring.

LONDON, Convent, 23 Kensington Square, W., boarding-school for young ladies; Poor School; Exposition of Blessed Sacrament daily from 8 o'clock Mass, until Benediction at 5 P.M.

RAMSGATE, Convent, Pegwell Road, West Cliff; boarding-school for children of the upper classes; lady boarders; exposition of the Blessed Sacrament, on Sundays and holidays, from 7 o'clock Mass, until Benediction at 5 P.M.

RICHMOND, Yorks, Priory of Our Lady of Peace; boarding-school for the education of young ladies; Poor Schools.

SIDMOUTH, Devon; education of children of delicate health; retreat for ladies throughout the year; Perpetual Adoration of the Blessed Sacrament.

Assumption (Little Sisters of the), Nursing Sisters of the Poor.

The members of this Community devote themselves exclusively and gratuitously, day and night, to the care of the sick poor in their own homes, irrespective of religious belief, cleaning and cooking for them, attending to their children, and becoming practically the servants of the poor, in order to win them to God. They accept nothing, not even food, from their patients, the poorest of whom have the first claim.

Their Mother House is at 57 Rue Violet, Paris.

Rule of St. Augustine.

Habit.—Black, with black veil.

Six of the Sisters came from France to England in 1880.

LONDON, 14 Wellington Road, Bow, E.; 42 St. James's Square, Notting Hill, W.

Augustine, St., English Canonesses Regular of Lateran (of the Perpetual Adoration).

Existed in England previous to the dissolution. An English Convent of the Order was established 1609, at Louvain, in Belgium. In 1794, in consequence of the French Revolution, they came to England, taking up their abode first at Hammersmith, and next, in the same year, at Amesbury Abbey, Wilts, and Spetisbury House, Co. Dorset. Removed, 2nd October 1861, to their present residence at Newton Abbot. From the period of their arrival in England until 1860, the Canonesses conducted a school for young ladies; they then (under rescript from Pius IX., dated 15th March 1860) established in their Convent the Perpetual Adoration of the Blessed Sacrament.

Rule of St. Augustine. Their church is never left without an adorer. Daily Exposition of the Blessed Sacrament from early Mass until Benediction at 7 P.M.; and, on the eves of great feasts, throughout the night.

Habit.—White woollen, with white linen rochet peculiar to the Canonesses of St. Augustine, a black veil, and a red cloth or woollen scapular, with a badge representing the Monstrance, surrounded by the words, "Praised, adored, and glorified be Jesus for ever, in the Adorable Sacrament of the Altar."

Newton Abbot, Devon, St. Augustine's Priory.

South Mimms, near Barnet, Herts, St. Monica's Priory, founded 1886, from St. Augustine's, Newton Abbot.

Augustine, St. (Canonesses Regular of Lateran).

Haywards Heath, Sussex, Priory of Our Lady of Good Counsel (1886). In 1629 the English Monastery of Canonesses Regular of Lateran, at Louvain, sent out a colony to found a house in Bruges. These devoted themselves to the work of education, which was interrupted by the French Revolution, when the Community took refuge in England. Returning to Bruges in 1802, they have ever since continued to educate girls, and in 1886 they founded this house at Haywards Heath, where the great duty of the Divine Office is carried on, and where a limited number of pupils are received.

Rule of St. Augustine, with Constitutions of the ancient C.C.R.R. of Windesheim.

Habit.—White cloth, linen rochet, black veil, surplice on great feasts; black cloth mantle in winter.

Augustine (Nuns of St.)

Founded in 1841 by Very Rev. Canon Maes, at Bruges.

Objects.—The care and treatment of persons of both sexes suffering from mental maladies,

and of children of weak intellect, or afflicted with idiotcy. Open to all denominations. Mother House, St. Julien's Hospice, Bruges.
Rule of St. Augustine.

BURGESS HILL, Sussex, Convent, St. George's Retreat. Treatment of mental maladies in both sexes.

Benedictine Nuns.

St. Benedict did not write a second Rule for women, when he became the master of the spiritual life of his sister, St. Scholastica, during the years she dwelt in a Convent at Piombariola, about five miles from Monte Cassino. From the very beginning of the Order, as the sons of St. Benedict passed into different lands, Monasteries of women were either founded or put themselves under the Rule, the same as that of the Monks. England, which became so thoroughly Benedictine, had numerous houses of Nuns of this Order. Towards the close of the sixteenth century some English ladies founded a Benedictine Convent for English subjects at Brussels. These Nuns are contemplatives. The public solemnisation of the Divine Office has a prominent place in their daily service. In some houses they have schools, as the Rule of St. Benedict allows the admission of children within the enclosure for the sake of education.

Rule.—That of St. Benedict. Vows perpetual. Enclosed.

Habit.—Black tunic, scapular, and veil, with white veilette, wimple, and fillet. In choir the cowl or great habit is worn. Abbesses wear a pectoral cross and abbatial ring, and use a crozier.

The Benedictine houses of Nuns in England are classed under two heads—I. those incorporated in some Congregation; II. those that are self-contained, and subject to the Ordinary.

I.

STANBROOK, near Worcester, St. Mary's Abbey (education of young ladies), belonging to the Anglo-Benedictine Congregation.

In 1623 the Monks of the English Benedictine Congregation founded an English Nunnery at Cambray, belonging to their own Congregation, and wholly subject thereto, instead of to the Ordinary. The Nuns ultimately, after imprisonment at Compiègne, returned to England in 1795, and established themselves successively at Woolton, near Liverpool; at Abbot's Salford, in Warwickshire, in 1807; and in 1838 at Stanbrook.

MINSTER-IN-THANET, near Ramsgate. St. Mildred's Convent, belongs to the Cassinese Congregation.

II.

ATHERSTONE, Warwickshire, St. Scholastica's Priory. A Community of Benedictine

Nuns, with the Perpetual Adoration of the Most Blessed Sacrament. They are strictly enclosed, and have no schools. The Community was an affiliation from St. Benedict's Priory, near Colwich, in May 1859.

COLWICH, St. Benedict's Priory. A filiation was made from Cambray to Paris in 1652, from where, after suffering great hardships from the Revolution, they arrived in London in July 1795. At first they settled at Marnhull, Dorset, removing successively in 1807 to Cannington, near Bridgwater, and in 1835 to their present house at Colwich. At Cannington they were the first to establish in England, in 1829, the Perpetual Adoration of the Blessed Sacrament.

DUMFRIES, N.B., of Perpetual Adoration.

EAST BERGHOLT, Suffolk. Monastery of the Glorious Assumption, St. Mary's Abbey. The Benedictine Monastery for Nuns, founded at Brussels in 1598, under the title of the Glorious Assumption of the Blessed Virgin Mary, was the first Monastery erected for English subjects after the destruction of religious houses by Henry VIII.

The foundresses of this Abbey were Lady Mary Percy, and the two sisters, Dorothy and Gertrude Arundel.

The first Abbess was Dame Joanna Berkeley, daughter of Sir John Berkeley of Beveston Castle, Gloucestershire. Lady Mary Percy succeeded her as second Abbess in 1616.

The French Revolution forced the Nuns to leave Belgium in 1794, all the property, papers, and records being confiscated by the French. They settled first at Winchester, where they were received and assisted by Dr. Milner, at that time priest of the mission in that town. In 1857 they removed to East Bergholt, in Suffolk, where they built a conventual church. In 1877 the Community relinquished their school, on account of the great number of educational establishments now in England, and also because they desired to have no hindrance to that chief duty which St. Benedict enjoins upon his Order—the public praise of God in choir. Labour, mental and manual, as enforced by the same holy Rule, fills up the intervening hours of the day.

OULTON, near Stone, Staffordshire, St. Mary's Abbey (school for young ladies). A filiation from Brussels was founded at Ghent in 1624, from which place they came to England at the French Revolution, settling in 1795 at Preston, in 1811 at Caverswall Castle, near Stone, Staffordshire, and in 1854 at Oulton.

PRINCETHORPE, near Rugby, St. Mary's Priory. These Nuns are the representatives of the Benedictine Convent of Montargis, diocese of Orleans, which Community came originally from Montmartre, near Paris, whose oundress was Mother Mary Grainger. To the school of Montargis came not only the children of France, but also those of the persecuted English aristocracy. This fact afterwards influenced in a remarkable manner the destiny of the Community. In 1792, seeing there was no safety for them in France, they embarked from Dieppe for Brighton on March 16th, 1792, and landed at Shoreham, proceeding to Brighton, where they were met by the Prince of Wales, afterwards George IV., to whom, through Mrs. Fitzherbert, representations had been made by families whose children had been educated at Montargis. By him and these friends they were treated with the greatest respect and hospitality; and on their telling the Prince that they intended to go to Holland, he said, "Stay where you are; I will protect you."

At Rodney Hall, Norfolk, they first resumed their community and educational life. On account of the growing numbers, they were obliged to remove to Heath Hall, in Yorkshire. In 1833 they bought the land of Princethorpe, and there erected the present buildings.

TEIGNMOUTH, Devon, St. Scholastica's Abbey. Founded in 1662 at Dunkirk, by a filiation from the English Benedictine Convent

SISTERS OF BON SECOURS.

at Ghent. They remained in possession of their Convent until the French Revolution broke out, when, in October 1793, they were expelled, and remained prisoners for eighteen months in the Convent of the Poor Clares at Gravelines. In 1795 they obtained leave from the English Government to return to England; and in May of the same year they settled at Hammersmith, where they remained until 1863, when they removed to Teignmouth. In 1875 the Perpetual Adoration was established, their school for young ladies having been previously given up.

VENTNOR, Isle of Wight, Priory of the Sacred Heart. This is an offshoot from the Abbaye de Notre Dame de la Paix, Liége. In the summer of 1882 the Benedictines of Liége purchased the beautiful property of Steephill View, Ventnor, in one of the most lovely spots of the Undercliffe, and opened their present boarding-school for young ladies. The Nuns are of various nationalities, thus offering to pupils the advantages of a Continental and an English education without leaving the country. They follow the Rule of St. Benedict, together with the Declarations of the Congregations of Beuron and Solesmes.

Bon Secours, Sisters of (du Notre Dame).

Founded in 1824 by the Archbishop of Paris, Monseigneur Hyacinthe Louis de Quélen.

Introduced of late years into the United Kingdom. Mother House and Novitiate, 20 Rue Notre Dame des Champs, Paris.

Object.—Care of the sick, rich or poor, in their own homes, without distinction of creed.

Rule of St. Ignatius. Are enjoined six hours' sleep a day when attending the sick.

Habit.—Black; white frilled cap.

LONDON, Bayswater, 54 Norfolk Terrace, W.; besides eleven houses in France.

BELFAST, Clonard Lodge, 53 Falls Road.

CORK, Western Road.

DUBLIN, 64 Lower Mount Street.

TRALEE, Co. Kerry.

Bon Secours, Sisters of (from Troyes).

Founded in 1840 by Abbé Millet, Canon of the Cathedral at Troyes. Nurse the sick in their own homes throughout the United Kingdom. Mother House and Novitiate at Troyes. One hundred and fifteen houses of the Congregation spread over Europe, seven in Africa, one in New York.

Habit.—Black; white headdress, black veil, brass crucifix attached to a violet braid.

The Congregation, the Rule of which was drawn up by the founder, has been approved by the Holy See, and a branch house was opened in Rome in 1863. In time of war the Sisters nurse the soldiers on the battlefield and in the ambulances. In Africa during several epidemics, and whilst the cholera raged in France, they counted many victims amongst those who sacrificed themselves in the service of the stricken ones.

LONDON, 21 Maitland Park Villas, Haverstock Hill, N.W. All applications for Sisters to be made to the Sister Superior, as above.

Bridgettine Nuns, or of our Saviour.

Founded in 1344 in Sweden by St. Bridget of Sweden, for special devotion to the Passion of our Lord and the honour of His Holy Mother. Established at Sion House, on the Thames, by Henry V. in 1414. Retired at the dissolution to Dermond, in Flanders; recalled to Sion House by Queen Mary in 1557; left again for Dermond in 1559, on accession of Elizabeth; removed next to Zierickzee, in Zeeland, Antwerp, Malines, and Rouen; and in 1594 settled at Lisbon. In 1810, owing to the French Revolution, some of the Community came back to England, and, being in passing difficulties, established a ladies' school at Peckham, removing afterwards to Newcastle-on-Tyne and Stowe; otherwise the Order is a purely contemplative one, its distinguishing features being prayer and fasting. This branch becoming extinct, the remainder of the Lisbon Community returned to their native England in 1861, and took up their residence at Spetisbury. They are now building a new Monastery, to be called St. Bridget's Abbey of Sion, at Chudleigh, South Devon, which they will take possession of as soon as completed.

Rule of St. Augustine, with special constitutions added, confirmed by Martin V. in the fifteenth century.

Habit of iron-gray, with (in choir) a cowl and mantle. On the head, a black veil and a white linen crown, upon which are sewed five pieces of red cloth in form of a cross, in memory of the Crown of Thorns and the five wounds of our Lord.

SPETISBURY, near Blandford, Dorset. After 1886 St. Bridget's Abbey of Sion, Chudleigh, South Devon.

Brigid, St., Sisters of (Patroness of Ireland).

Founded in Tullow, Co. Carlow, by the Most Rev. Dr. Delaney, Bishop of Kildare and Leighlin, in 1807, for the special instruction of girls of the different classes of society.

Rule of St. Augustine, modified to suit the requirements of an institute devoted to education.

A peculiar feature of the Institute of St. Brigid is the teaching of the girls and adult-female portion of the Congregation in the parish churches adjoining the Convents, on Sundays and holidays, before each of the Masses and Vespers.

ABBEYLEIX, Queen's Co.

BALLYROAN, Queen's Co., branch from Abbeyleix.

GORESBRIDGE, Co. Kilkenny.

MOUNTRATH, Queen's Co.

PAULSTOWN, Co. Kilkenny, branch from Goresbridge.

TULLOW, Co. Carlow, Mother House (1807).

Carmelite Nuns.

Although claiming a higher antiquity, these Nuns were first constituted as they now exist by John Soreth, General of the Order, in 1452, and the Rule was approved by Nicholas V. in the same year. St. Teresa instituted a reform of this Order. Mother Anne of the Ascension, whose family name was Worsley, was the first Englishwoman who became a Carmelite of the Teresian reform. After being professed at Mons under the Spanish Mothers, who had lived with and received their instructions from St. Teresa herself, she made a foundation for the English at Antwerp, and this increasing in numbers, another English foundation was made at Lierre, and from here the Nuns came to England on 12th July 1794.

Rule.—Silence, fasting, and prayer. Cloistered. In Ireland, however, some of the houses have schools, but as a rule the life of Carmelite Nuns is essentially contemplative. Like the

Fathers, they are divided into calced and discalced. All the houses in England are discalced.

Habit.—Brown, with brown scapular. In choir, white cloak and black veil.

CHICHESTER, Sussex, Convent of Mount Carmel (Teresian). Were founded at Hoogstraet on the 18th of August 1678, by the Lady Mary Gabriel, widow of the Prince Salm Salm and Duke of Hoogstraet. On account of the wars in 1701 the Community were obliged to leave their Convent and go to Mechlin, from whence they returned to their Convent of Hoogstraet towards the end of the year 1712, where they remained till the French took the Low Countries in 1794, which caused all the English Religious to quit the country, and the Carmelites came to England. They removed to Canford House, Dorsetshire. In the year 1825, their means not allowing them to remain any longer in England, the Bishop allowed them, on condition that when they were able to return they would, to remove to France, where they settled at Valognes, in Normandy. In 1870 they returned to England, having bought land near Chichester, where they are now settled, and have built a Convent in the thirteenth century style.

DARLINGTON, Durham, Carmel House; Our Lady of Mount Carmel and St. Joseph;

Church of the Immaculate Conception, consecrated 25th October 1859. A colony of the same house (that of Lierre) as the one at Lanherne, went first in 1794 to Auckland, St. Helens; in 1804 to Cocken Hall, Durham; and finally in 1830 to Darlington (Teresians).

LANHERNE, St. Columb, Cornwall, founded in 1794, from Lierre (Teresians).

LONDON, Convent of the Most Holy Trinity, St. Charles's Square, Bayswater, W., founded 1878, from the Rue d'Enfer, Paris (Teresians); Mount Carmel Hermitage, Lillie Road, West Brompton, foundation from Lyons (Teresians).

WELLS, Carmelite Convent, The Vista (Teresians), foundation from Lanherne to Sclerder, 1864; transferred to Plymouth in 1871; thence to Wells in 1875.

DELGANY, Co. Wicklow, founded December 8th, 1844, by the Community of St. Teresa's Convent, Warren Mount, Dublin. The Convent has a Gothic church, and a school for the poor, attached to it, and is built on a hill adjoining the village. Its situation at the extremity of Kilquade parish, and adjoining those of Bray and Enniskerry, enables many persons who live far away from their parochial churches to attend all the exercises of religion with facility, the church being open to the public. It is also a privilege of this Convent that it was the first religious house founded in the Co. Wicklow since the Reformation.

DUBLIN, Ranelagh. Existed in Dublin in the year 1661—how long before is not known. The Community struggled through the penal times, sometimes gaining their livelihood by needlework, sometimes by lodgers, going through all their religious exercises together. Towards the beginning of this century the Community got a license from the Protestant Archbishop of Dublin to open a school for young ladies, which was at that time the only one of the kind in or near Dublin. By degrees, as the penal times passed away, the Nuns adopted the Carmelite habit. They also had a Poor School, which they attended. In 1830 the Community closed their schools, established grates, and embraced the reform of St. Teresa, which is now strictly observed. All the other Carmelite Convents in Dublin came from this house, either directly or from some of those houses which filiated from this.

KILMACUD, Stillorgan. Convent of Our Lady and St. Joseph. Founded 1881, with the approbation and under the patronage of his Eminence Cardinal McCabe, Archbishop of Dublin.

Rule is that of the reform of St. Teresa.

WARREN MOUNT, Mill Street, Convent of St. Teresa. This Convent of Teresian Carmelites was founded in 1813 by the Rev. Mother Clare (Lyons), a filiation from the ancient Carmelite Convent of St. Joseph's, Ranelagh, near Dublin. There being no provision at that time for the education of poor Catholic children, and the proselytising system actively carried on, it was deemed advisable to open a school for poor female children, which was done with the approbation of the Apostolic See, and still exists, attached to the Convent.

TRANQUILLA, Upper Rathmines, Carmel of the Nativity. A Community of the Discalced Carmelites.

BLACKROCK, Mount Carmel.

FIRHOUSE, Tallaght, Convent of the Assumption,

HAMPTON, Drumcondra, Monastery of the Incarnation.

ROEBUCK, Dundrum, Mount Carmel.

NEW ROSS, Co. Wexford, Carmelite Convent. Teresians, who came to this town from Dublin seventy years since, during which time the Community have conducted a well-attended Poor School, and lace-making apartment for adults.

Charity, Sisters of, of St. Vincent de Paul (Filles de la Charite).

Founded in Paris in 1633 by St. Vincent de Paul and Louise de Marillac, widow of Antoine le Gras. Laid the foundation of all modern religious Communities who lead an *active* life of charity. So obviously needed was this novel institution that the Holy See, which had hitherto refrained from countenancing all other attempts of a kindred character, solemnly approved of " the Daughters of Charity" in 1655. The Community, as finally constituted, was "to consist of girls, and widows unencumbered with children, destined to seek out the poor in the alleys and streets of cities. They were to have for monastery the houses of the sick; for cell, a hired room; for their chapel, the parish church; for their cloister, the streets of the town or the wards of the hospital; for enclosure, obedience; for grating, the fear of God; for veil, holy modesty."

The Daughters of Charity at this present time number between thirty and forty thousand Sisters, with two thousand houses in all parts of the globe, devoted to every conceivable work of charity. The Father-General of the Congregation of the Mission at Paris is the Superior of the Community, which is governed under him by the Superioress, who is elected every three years, and who resides at the Mother House, Rue de Bac, Paris. After five years' probation, the Sisters take simple vows, renewable every year.

Habit.—Gray-blue cloth, with large white collar, and white cornette for the head.

The Novitiate for Great Britain was opened in 1885. Before that time postulants had to make their entire novitiate in Paris; now they go there only for a short time before their clothing.

ST. VINCENT'S, Mill Hill, Middlesex, House of the English Novitiate, where the Father-Director and the Sister Visitatrice (or Provincial) usually reside. An Orphanage for infant workhouse-boys will be opened in 1887, when the one at present existing at Leyton will be transferred here.

BOSTON SPA, Yorkshire, Institution of St. John of Beverley for deaf and dumb. Founded 9th of June 1870, at Handsworth Woodhouse, by the Right Rev. Monsignor Canon de Haerne, D.D., Domestic Prelate of Leo XIII. and Deputy of the Belgian Chambers. This is the *only* place in England for training Catholic deaf-mutes; the boys are instructed in shoemaking, tailoring, printing, &c., and the girls are taught household and laundry work, plain and fancy needlework, &c. This most deserving and unique charity is entirely dependent upon voluntary contributions, having no endowment whatever.

BULLINGHAM, near Hereford, St. Elizabeth's School; orphanage and middle-schools for boys and girls; day-schools under Government.

DARLINGTON, St. Augustine's Schools; day-schools under Government; visit of the poor.

DOVER, St. Mary's, Eastbrook House; Convalescent Home; day-schools under Government; visit of the poor.

HEREFORD. Day-schools under Government; orphanages for boys and girls; visit of the poor.

LANARK. Hospital for patients of both sexes, founded by the Sisters, with the aid of Mr. Monteith of Carstairs. Among the comparatively small number of charitable institutions which the Catholics of Scotland can boast of, this hospital holds a prominent, if not the leading, position. The idea of this institution was first mooted some sixteen years ago, when a serious epidemic was raging in the town of Lanark. To grapple with the terrible disaster, the Sisters of Charity converted the little cottage they had into an hospital, and that small, but heroic, effort of the Sisters formed the nucleus of the present handsome erection in the town. The Sisters call the attention of the Catholic community to a feature in their work not to be met with in any other hospital, namely, the admittance of private patients. By this means, persons in a respectable position, but whose circumstances do not permit of their friends procuring them the trained nursing so necessary in cases of illness, can, on payment of a small weekly sum, have a private room and all the comforts of home, added to medical attendance and hospital nursing. Another feature is that their institution procures for patients not only help for the body, but also those spiritual aids which are of even greater moment. They can give many instances of careless and bad Christians, who have been brought to a sense of their religious duties or returned to a better life, as a result of their stay in the hospital. There is no fund or certain income to maintain Lanark Hospital. It depends on generous subscriptions and collections. It would be a great relief to those in charge of the institution if they could rely on an annual subscription-list, even if the individual amounts were small. Day-school under Government; middle-class boarding-school; visit of the poor.

SMYLLUM, Orphanage, Deaf-Mute and Blind Asylum. Orphanage founded 1864; Deaf-Mute and Blind Asylum, 1871; 400 orphans, 30 deaf-mutes, and 6 blind children in the institution. Needlework and point-lace executed by the orphan girls; fret and fancy wood work done by the boys, who are also taught carpentering, gardening, tailoring, shoemaking, and farm-service on the premises. Forty parochial boards send children to the orphanage; non-parochial children are supported by private charity.

LIVERPOOL:

Beacon Lane, industrial school for boys; visit of the poor.

Brunswick Road, Blind Asylum; visit of the poor.

60 Mason Street, St. Anne's certified Industrial School for Girls: opened June 1867; will be removed shortly to a new school at Freshfield, twelve miles from Liverpool, on a site given to the institution by Thomas Weld-Blundell, Esq., of Ince Blundell Hall. The children contribute to their own support by plain needlework, and by making ecclesiastical vestments, embroidery, and handwork of all kinds. A laundry is to be opened on the new premises.

Little Crosby, day-schools; visit of the poor.

LONDON:

Carlisle Place, Westminster, orphanage for girls; crèche for babies; day and night schools; mothers' meetings; visit of the poor.

9 and 11 Lower Seymour Street. The works carried on here by the Sisters are a crèche for infants; an orphanage of 150 children; a home for young girls in business, and pupil-teachers; a day-school for children of the middle class, a night-school for girls at work during the day; mothers' meetings, and relief of the poor. Besides these, the Sisters visit

the poor of two parishes at their own homes, and the sick in the hospitals, and have charge of a night-school for boys and young men in Marylebone Lane, and four associations of Children of Mary, who meet in their respective parishes every Sunday afternoon. A work-class is also established in the Convent, and the Sisters will be grateful if ladies will patronise it by giving under-linen, &c., to be done by the girls. The institution has no funds, and depends for its support on voluntary contributions.

Clerkenwell Road, Hatton Garden, day-schools under Government; visit of the poor.

Queen Square, Bloomsbury, Italian Hospital, founded in 1884 by the exertions of Cavaliere Ortelli. A very considerable number of the sick poor who have been relieved would, but for the Italian Hospital, certainly have suffered more, and perhaps perished in this country. Most of the Italian poor have little knowledge of English habits and customs, and when taken ill they become abandoned in their miserable homes. But although the Hospital was established for Italians, it nevertheless opens its doors to persons of all nations and creeds.

MANCHESTER, Victoria Park, St. Joseph's Industrial School for Girls.

NEWCASTLE-ON-TYNE, Ashburton House, Gosforth, industrial school for girls.

PLYMOUTH, St. Teresa's Orphanage, for boys and girls; visit of the poor.

SALISBURY, St. Elizabeth's Industrial School for Girls. This establishment was started in 1871 through the generosity of its principal benefactress, Lady Herbert of Lea, who purchased the house and premises, to which were added, two years ago, a large well-fitted laundry, and another old house and garden. The children are either from the workhouse, or are voluntary cases, and are received between the ages of six and thirteen, until they are sixteen and seventeen. They are educated in the schools, and are trained in laundry and needlework. Very good situations are procured for them when they leave, unless their parents wish to have them home. Their own work supports a great many of the girls who receive no payment. Very few annual subscriptions are added to the sum Lady Herbert gives every year.

SHEFFIELD:

Howard Hill, St. Joseph's Home; reformatory for girls; day-school under Government.

Red Hill, day-schools, under Government; night-schools; visit of the poor.

Kirk Edge, Oughtibridge, industrial school for girls.

DUBLIN, North William Street, St. Vincent de Paul's girls' orphanage, and extern Poor-Schools; visit of the poor.

The Sisters of Charity were called to Dublin by the Most Rev. Dr. Cullen in 1857. The works confided to them were, at that time, to visit the sick poor, and to teach the Poor-Schools, which are unconnected with the National Board. There are four large school-rooms for the extern poor children, one of them being for infant boys and girls under seven years of age. The number of children attending the schools is 600. The orphanage was founded in December 1858. The object of this charity is to save poor orphan girls, and to train them to become useful servants. Since the foundation, over 500 have been provided with good situations.

There are at present in the institution about 180 orphans, who depend for their support on voluntary contributions. The orphans contribute to their own support by their work, and orders are thankfully received for needle-work, or more especially for artificial flowers.

Convent Avenue, Fairview, St. Vincent's Asylum for the cure of mental diseases. This institution having been founded for the reception of female patients of the respectable and educated classes of society having only limited means, they are admitted at moderate, although inadequate, payments. For other patients the pensions vary, according to circumstances.

Cork, North Infirmary.

Drogheda, industrial school for boys; day-school under Government; visit of the poor.

Charity of Refuge (Sisters of Our Lady of).

Founded in 1641 by the Ven. John Eudes at Caen, in Normandy, for the reclamation of women who have fallen, or are in danger of falling, into a vicious life.

Rule of St. Augustine, with special constitutions. Enclosed.

Bartestree, Hereford, Convent of Our Lady of Charity of Refuge.

Waterlooville, Hants.

Drumcondra, near Dublin, St. Mary's Asylum and Reformatory; Convent, High Park. This institution, founded in 1853 by Rev. John Smith, provides for 130 penitent females. A reformatory for juvenile offenders has been under care of the Sisters since 1859, and contains over 70 girls.

Charity, Sisters of (of St. Paul the Apostle).

Founded in 1700 by the Abbé Louis Chauvet, Curé of Levéville la Chenard, aided by Marie de Tylly and Mdlle. Dutrouchon. Dispersed at the Revolution, and restored by Napoleon. The English branch came to Banbury in 1847. They are a teaching Order. The Mother House is at Chartres; the head house for England is at St. Paul's Convent, Selley Oak, Birmingham.

AVON-DASSETT, Warwickshire, St. Joseph; one mixed and one middle-class boarding-school.

BANBURY, Oxford, St. John's; two mixed, two infant, and one boarding school.

BATLEY, Yorkshire, St. Mary's; two mixed and infant schools.

BIRMINGHAM, St. Chad; three girls, infant, and select schools. St. Michael, three girls, infant, and night schools. St. John, two girls and infant schools. St. Joseph, two girls and infant schools.

BLACKHILL, Durham, St. Mary; two mixed and infant schools.

BRADFORD, St. Patrick; three mixed, infant, and select schools.

BROOMS, Durham, SS. Mary and Joseph; two mixed and infant schools.

BROWNEDGE, Lancashire, St. Benedict; three mixed, infant, and select schools.

BOSTON, St. Mary; one mixed school.

CAMPDEN, Gloucestershire, SS. Peter and Paul; one mixed school.

CHELTENHAM, St. Gregory; two mixed and infant schools.

CLEATOR, St. Mary; two mixed and infant schools.

CLEATOR MOOR, two mixed and infant schools.

CONSETT, St. Patrick; two mixed and infant schools.

COLESHILL, St. Paul; home for workhouse boys (certified).

COSSEY, Norwich, St. Augustine; two mixed and infant schools.

CROOK, St. Cuthbert; two mixed and infant schools.

DARLINGTON, St. William; two mixed and infant schools.

DUDLEY, three mixed, infant, and select schools.

EVERINGHAM, St. Everilda; one mixed school.

EXTON, St. Francis of Assisi; one mixed school.

GARSTANG, St. Michael; two mixed and infant schools.

GLOSSOP, St. Paul; one mixed school.

GREAT CROSBY, SS. Peter and Paul; two mixed and infant schools.

HADFIELD, St. Joseph; one mixed school.

HAMPTON WICK, Sacred Heart of Jesus; two mixed and infant schools.

HOLYWELL, St. Winefride; three mixed, infant, and boarding schools.

HOWARD TOWN, St. Mary; one infant school.

KENDAL, St. Mary; two mixed and infant schools.

LEAMINGTON, St. Peter; two girls and infant schools.

LEEDS, St. Patrick; two girls and infant schools. St. Anne, three girls, infant, and select schools.

MARYPORT, St. John; two mixed and infant schools.

NEWCASTLE-ON-TYNE, St. Andrew; two mixed and infant schools.

NORTH STOCKTON-ON-TEES, St. Mary; two girls and infant schools. St. Patrick, one mixed school.

RADFORD, St. Mary; two mixed and middle-class boarding-school.

RAINHILL, Prescot, St. Mary; two mixed and infant schools.

SEAHAM HARBOUR, St. Francis of Sales; one mixed school.

SOUTHPORT, St. Mary; two mixed and infant schools. Little Ireland, one mixed school.

STOURBRIDGE, St. Joseph; three mixed, infant, and select schools.

STUDLEY, St. Mary; two mixed and infant schools.

THORNDON, Our Lady and St. Laurence; one mixed school.

WAKEFIELD, St. Joseph; two mixed and infant schools.

WHITEHAVEN, St. Anne; two mixed and infant schools.

WHITWICK, Holy Cross; two mixed and infant schools.

WOOLTON, St. Mary; two mixed and infant schools.

WORCESTER, St. George; three mixed, infant, and select schools.

WORKINGTON, St. Michael; two mixed and infant schools.

YORK, St. Wilfrid; two mixed and infant schools.

Charity (Irish Sisters of).

Founded at Dublin in 1815 by Mary Francis Aikenhead, under the auspices of Dr. Murray, Archbishop of Dublin. The Congregation was approved by the Holy See in 1834. The Superioress, who resides at Harold's Cross, Dublin, has jurisdiction over all the members of the Community,

Rule.—Of St. Ignatius, with suitable modifications. The vows are perpetual. After two years and a half probation subjects are admitted to the *habit.*

BALLAGHADEREEN, sick mission, 450 poor children.

BENADA, sick mission, 250 poor children.

CLARENBRIDGE, Oranmore, Co. Galway.

CLONMEL, Co. Tipperary, Convent of SS. Peter and Paul; orphanage for 32 children Poor Schools, with 500.

CORK:

Convent of St. Patrick, Wellington Road (1870), with Hospital for Incurables, men, women, and children.

Convent of St. Vincent de Paul, Peacock Lane, with Magdalen Asylum for 100 penitents; sick mission; Poor Schools, with about 700 children.

DUBLIN:

Baldoyle (1869), religious instruction in the parochial schools; visiting the sick poor.

Blackrock, Grove Avenue, Convalescent Home of St. Vincent's Hospital in Stephen's Green.

Donnybrook, Asylum of St. Mary Magdalen (1798), for 100 penitents; Poor Schools.

Fairview, Asylum of St. Vincent, for cure of mental diseases, Convent Avenue.

Gardiner Street (Upper) Poor Schools, with 800 girls.

Harold's Cross, large Poor Schools; Hospice for the Dying, Our Lady's Mount, accommodation for 41 patients.

Merrion, St. Mary's Female Blind Asylum, for 350 inmates; situated in a demesne of thirty-three acres; certified industrial school.

Milltown, Co. Dublin, Convent of Mount St. Anne; residence of Superior-General.

Mountjoy Street, Orphanage of St. Joseph, founded 1770; 100 inmates. King's Inns Street Schools, where 1000 pupils attend.

Sandymount, Convent of the Immaculate Conception; over 100 orphans, &c.

Stanhope Street, St. Mary's Industrial Training School (1819), for children of respectable parents or orphans, who are provided for in every respect during their residence; sick poor visited and relieved; orphans, 127.

St. Lawrence Place, new Convent attached to St. Lawrence O'Toole's; sick poor visited, and religious instruction in parochial schools; 800 children.

St. Stephen's Green (East), St. Vincent's Hospital, for 140 patients, opened by the Sisters in 1834.

Temple Street (Upper), 15, Hospital of St. Joseph, for sick children, founded 1872 (removed from Buckingham Street, May 1879).

KILKENNY, industrial school; visiting the sick and poor.

TRAMORE, Co. Waterford, founded 1866; sick mission; schools, with 250 children.

WATERFORD, Orphanage for 70 children; Poor Schools, with 600.

Christian Retreat (Sisters of the).

Founded in 1797, at Les Fontenelles, by Père Antoine Céleste Receveur, who was declared Venerable by Leo XIII., May 8th, 1883. The Society was approved by Pius VII. and Pius IX. The members are not bound by vows, a solemn promise taking their place. They have no revenue, supporting themselves by their own work. They devote themselves to education and giving spiritual retreats.

Their dress consists of habit, scapular, and coif of cream-coloured serge. First established in England, at Peckham, in 1848, under protection of Cardinal Wiseman. They entered their present house in May 1865; and the numbers of the Community increasing, a new chapel was built in 1885, which is served by a priest belonging to the same Community.

LONDON, Convent of St. Joseph, South Lambeth, S.W.; boarding-school for young ladies; Clayland's Road, day-school for poor children; spiritual retreats.

Cistercian Nuns.

Founded by St. Bernard (whose sister Humbeline was one of the earliest members) in 1128, as an Order of Nuns corresponding to the Cistercian Monks, at the Abbey of Tart, in the diocese of Langres, and were at first known under the name of Bernardines. Came to England in 1801, having been previously located at La Sainte Volonté de Dieu, in the Bas Valais, Switzerland, until the French Revolution, and then successively in Germany, Poland, and White Russia.

Rule of St. Benedict. Contemplation, manual labour, singing of Divine Office. Silence, vigils, and perpetual abstinence from meat, fowl, fish, &c.

Habit.—White.

STAPEHILL, Wimborne, Dorset, Convent of Our Lady of Dolours (1847); church consecrated 16th July 1851. Poor School attached. Stapehill was presented to the Nuns by the eighth Lord Arundell of Wardour in November 1802; previously to which they had been resident for short periods after their arrival in England at Hammersmith, and at Burton, near Christchurch.

Congregation of Jesus and Mary.

Founded soon after the Reign of Terror, by Claudine Thévenet and the Abbé Coindre, at Fourvières, Lyons, for the education of girls. The Rule and Constitution, were approved by the Holy See in 1847.

IPSWICH, Albion Hill, Convent of Jesus and Mary, a branch of the Mother House at

Fourvières, and was founded in 1847. There are three schools—(1) a boarding-school for young ladies; (2) an orphanage, certified by Local Government Board; (3) a Poor School.

LONDON, Willesden, N.W., Convent of Jesus and Mary; boarding and day school for young ladies; middle-class school.

Congregation of the Daughters of the Cross.

Founded at Liége, September 8th, 1833. The Institute was approved by the Holy See in 1845, and the Constitutions in 1851. It is composed of choir Sisters and lay Sisters, and governed by a Superioress-General, who resides at the Mother House at Liége. After a two years' novitiate the Sisters are incorporated into the Congregation, first by temporary and then by perpetual vows.

The end of the Institute is the glory of God and the sanctification of the Sisters, by means of external works of charity performed in an interior spirit. No work of mercy of whatever kind is considered foreign to the spirit of the Institute.

BURY, Lancashire, St. Joseph's Convent, Manchester Road, founded May 1878; boarding-school for young ladies; higher grade elementary school; St. Mary's parish elementary schools.

LONDON:
St. Wilfrid's Convent, Cale Street, Chelsea, London, S.W., founded August 1869; boarding-school for young ladies; day-schools; Oratory parish schools for girls and infants; St. Ann's Orphanage; certified Poor Law school for girls.

St. Joseph's Orphanage, Kensington Hall, West Kensington, London, S.W., founded in September 1880, to be transferred in June 1887 to Totteridge, Herts; certified Poor Law school for girls.

MARGATE, Convent of the Holy Family, Grosvenor Place, founded June 1879; Convalescent Home for children and adults of different classes, in connection with the establishments at Chelsea and West Kensington.

Dames Augustine of the Immaculate Heart of Mary.

Object.—To afford a quiet and comfortable residence, for a time or permanently, to ladies of delicate health requiring special care; and, as boarders, to ladies desirous of a retired life.

LONDON, Kensington, Convent (du Saint Cœur de Marie), 10 Melbury Road, W., for ladies in delicate health and lady boarders.

Dames de Marie.

Founded in 1817, at Alost, Belgium, by Canon Van Crombrugghe, for female education.

CROYDON (West), Surrey, Coloma House, Tavistock Park, Bedford Road, for the higher education of young ladies.

SCARBOROUGH, Convent; boarding-school for young ladies.

Dames de Nazareth.

Founded in 1822, at Montmirail, Maine, by the Duchesse de la Rochefoucauld-Doudeauville, for the purpose of giving young ladies a solid and Christian education, combined with the usual accomplishments. Received the blessing of Pius IX. in 1875. They have five houses in the Holy Land, the most important being at Nazareth. Came to England in 1880.

SOUTH EALING, Middlesex, Convent ¶ of Nazareth, Ealing Park, W., exclusively devoted to the higher education of young ladies.

Dames Religieuses de la Croix.

Founded in 1625 by Rev. Pierre Guérin, Curé of Roye, in Picardy. Introduced into England in 1871.

Object.—Education of young ladies, with Poor Schools when practicable.

Rule of St. Ignatius.

BOURNEMOUTH, Hants, Convent, The Lodge, Mineham. Higher-class boarding-school for young ladies.

Dames de la Retraite (Society of Mary).

Founded in Brittany, 1660, by the Abbé de Kerlévio and Mdlle. de Francheville.

Rule of St. Ignatius. The Mother House is at Angers. Introduced into England in 1880.

CLAPHAM PARK, S.W., Convent, Atkins Road, board and education of young ladies.

Dames de la Mère de Dieu.

BRISTOL, Convent, Clifton Wood, Clifton; nursing Sisters, nurse the sick at their own homes; also priests in any part of England, with permission of the Bishop of the diocese; provide accommodation for priests in ill-health; receive lady boarders; visit the poor.

Dames de St. André.

Founded early in the present century at Tournai, in Belgium, by Madame Flavie Delattre, under patronage of the Bishop of Tournai, and consists of choir Nuns and lay Sisters. The Mother House is at Tournai, on the site of the ancient Monastery of St. André, whence their name.

Rule of St. Ignatius, which was approved for them by the Holy See, 14th April 1857. Is governed by a Mother-General, elected for life by the Community. Each house is under the jurisdiction of the Ordinary. The works of the Society are the education and instruction of young pupils, boarders or externs; training-schools, Poor Schools; spiritual retreats for ladies of the world.

Habit.—Black, with white muslin cap and collar.

JERSEY, St. Helier, where all classes of society receive instruction. The children are divided into four sections, according to their social position. On Sunday the work of Congregations is established, so as to be able to watch over and guide the young girls who have left school. St. Matthew's, at a seaside village six miles distant from St. Helier, a country mission for the instruction of the poor.

Daughters of the Faithful Virgin.

Founded in 1830, at La Delivrande, Calvados, the Mother House, by Henriette de Forestier d'Osseville, daughter of Count Théodore d'Osseville.

Object.—The maternal adoption of female orphans and other destitute children, who receive a Christian education, are taught to earn their living, and are always readmitted in case of necessity; also the education of rich and poor, the giving of spiritual retreats, &c.

Rule of St. Ignatius.

FOLKESTONE, Convent, Dover Street, for the superior education of young ladies, and as a residence for lady boarders.

NORWOOD (Upper), S.E., Surrey, for the

higher education of young ladies; orphanage school, certified by Poor Law Board, for reception of Catholic workhouse children. Attached to the orphanage is a home for the girls educated there, from which servants can be obtained.

Dominicanesses (of the Second Order of St. Dominic).

Founded about 1215, by St. Dominic; approved by Pope Honorius III. Established in 1661 as an English Convent at Vilvorde, near Brussels, by Father Philip Thomas (afterwards Cardinal) Howard. They removed in 1690 to Brussels, and in 1794 came over at the French Revolution to London, taking up their residence in the same year at Hartpury Court, near Gloucester, and afterwards, in 1839, at The Rosary, Atherstone, in Warwickshire; in June 1858 at Hurst Green, near Whalley, in Lancashire; and in December 1866 at their present residence, the gift of the Countess Clare, at Carisbrooke, in the Isle of Wight. Are under the Provincial of the English Province, and the General of the Order.

Rule of St. Augustine. Contemplative; cloistered.

Habit.—White, with white scapular and black veil for choir Nuns; black, with white veil, for lay Sisters.

CARISBROOKE, Newport, Isle of Wight, Convent of Our Lady of Reparation (1866).

BELFAST, St. Mary's Dominican Convent; boarding, day, and national schools.

BLACKROCK, Co. Dublin, Convent of St. Catherine (founded 1836), Sion Hill, with boarding and day schools.

CABRA, near Dublin, Convent of St. Mary, with boarding-schools; Poor Schools, and a deaf and dumb asylum, with over 200 inmates. The Nuns of Cabra, originally from the Galway house, came to Dublin in 1717. They have been at Cabra since 1819.

DROGHEDA, Siena Convent of St. Catherine, founded in 1722. Boarding, day, and poor schools. This Convent possesses the celebrated relic of the head of Oliver Plunkett, the martyred Archbishop of Armagh.

DUBLIN, Convent of Our Lady of Sion, 18 and 19 Eccles Street; day-school for young ladies. Attached to Convent in Eccles Street is a charitable institution, supported by voluntary contributions, for the maintenance, higher education, and advancement in life of the orphan daughters of those who have suffered by reverse of fortune.

GALWAY, Convent of Jesus and Mary, Mount St. Joseph, Taylor's Hill, established in Galway in 1644; boarding and day schools for young ladies.

KINGSTOWN, Co. Dublin, Convent of St.

Mary; was founded from Cabra in 1847. The Sisters are engaged in the education of children, rich and poor. They have a boarding-school and a day-school for young ladies, and a national school attended by 1000 children. The more destitute of these receive food and clothing at the Convent.

WICKLOW, Convent of St. Mary, a filiation of Kingstown.

Dominican Nuns (Third Order, or Tertiaries).

Objects.—A combination of the active and contemplative. Visit hospitals, the sick in their own homes, &c.

Rule.—Are bound by the three vows. Not enclosed.

STONE, Staffordshire, Convent of St. Dominic; St. Mary's Hospital for Incurables; boarding-school for the higher education of young ladies; Poor Schools for young boys, girls, and infants; and a work-school for young women. Visitation of the sick and poor. This Convent is the Mother House and Central Novitiate of the Congregation of St. Catherine of Siena, which includes the three undermentioned houses.

LONDON, Bow, Convent of St. Catherine of Siena (Broadway, E.); boarding school for young ladies; mixed Poor School and infant school; middle day-pension; visit of the poor and sick.

STOKE-ON-TRENT, Staffordshire, Convent of Our Lady of Angels, with St. Margaret's Hospital, for female patients afflicted with incurable diseases, who here secure a happy home for life; Poor School for girls and infants; and middle day-pension.

TORQUAY, Devon, Priory of St. Mary, St. Mary Church, with Poor Schools and female orphanage, and boarding-school for young ladies; a Guest House, in which ladies are received as boarders; retreats for ladies given during the summer months. The other Dominican houses are unconnected with the above.

CLIFTON, Bristol, Convent of St. Catherine, Park Place.

HARROW-ON-THE-HILL, Middlesex, Convent of St. Dominic.

KILBURN, N.W., Convent, Mutrix Road; boarding and day school for young ladies; day-school for young gentlemen.

NEWCASTLE-ON-TYNE, Northumberland, Convent of St. Dominic (1879); Poor Schools.

SOUTHSEA, Hants, Convent, Pelham Lodge, Pelham Road; day-school for young ladies, ditto for young gentlemen; visit poor and sick.

STROUD, near Woodchester, Gloucester, Convent of St. Rose; boarding-school for young ladies; also for children of the working classes.

WATFORD, Herts, Convent; and boarding-school for middle classes.

WEST GRINSTEAD, Sussex, Priory of St. Dominic.

Dominican Sisters of Penance (of Third Order of St. Dominic).

HINCKLEY, Leicester.

LEICESTER, with boarding-school for girls.

Faithful Companions of Jesus.

Founded in 1820 at Amiens, by Madame Marie-Madeleine Victoire de Bonnault d'Houet (*née* de Bengy). Approved by Leo XII. in August 1826, and confirmed by Gregory XVI. in August 1837.

Object.—Devotion to female education. Mother House in Paris. Introduced into England in November 1830, when, under Madame d'Houet, they took charge, on their own system, of extensive schools at Somers Town, previously established by the Abbé Carron.

BIRKENHEAD, Cheshire, Convent, Tranmere Hall, Holt Hill, near Woodside Ferry; boarding and day school for young ladies.

CHESTER, Convent, Dee House; boarding-school for young ladies, the course of studies comprising all the branches of an accomplished education.

Exeter, Devon, Convent, Holloway House, Holloway; boarding-school for young ladies; Poor Schools.

Isleworth, Middlesex, Convent, Gumley House (opened 25th March 1841); first-class boarding-school, with Poor Schools attached.

Liverpool, Convent, 1, 2, and 3 Great George Square; boarding-school for the higher education of young ladies; also elementary schools at St. Patrick's and Our Lady of Mount Carmel.

London, Howrah House, East India Dock Road, Poplar, E.; boarding and day schools for young ladies.

Somers Town, N.W., Convent, Clarendon Square; middle-class boarding-school of St. Aloysius (1843); young ladies' day-school.

Manchester, Convent, 130 Upper Brook Street; St. Augustine's public elementary school and boarding-school.

Middlesbrough, Convent of St. Mary's, Gunnergate Terrace; boarding-school for young ladies; training-school for pupil-teachers.

Pendleton, Salford, Lancashire; public elementary school of Mother of God and St. James.

Preston, Lancashire, Convent, Lark Hill House; boarding-school for young ladies; elementary schools at St. Augustine's.

REDCAR, Convent of St. Hilda; school for young ladies (boarders and day-pupils) at Coatham; Poor School.

SALFORD, Lancashire, Convent, Adelphi House, Crescent; boarding and high schools; public elementary schools, Chimeson Street, Craven Street, and Sussex Street.

SKIPTON, Convent of St. Monica; higher education of young ladies; Poor Schools.

UPTON HALL, near Birkenhead, Convent, Upton Hall (formerly Lingdale House); boarding-school for young ladies.

BRUFF, Co. Limerick.

LIMERICK, Convent, Laura Hill (1844); first-class boarding and day schools.

NEWTOWNBARRY, Co. Wexford. School for young ladies.

Franciscans (Third Order Regular).

Founded by St. Francis of Assisi. St. Elizabeth of Hungary, being the first woman known to have taken the three vows in this Order, is considered its principal patroness. Each house is independent, except those specially mentioned as filiations.

ABERDEEN, N.B., Convent of the Immaculate Conception, Huntly Street.

BOTHWELL, Lanark, N.B., Convent at Elmwood.

FRANCISCANS.

EDINBURGH, N.B., Convent, Albany Street, filiation from Glasgow.

GLASGOW, N.B., Convent of the Immaculate Conception, 72 Abercromby Street, with certified industrial school for boys and girls.

Convent of the Immaculate Conception, 58 Charlotte Street.

GREENOCK, N.B., Convent of the Immaculate Conception, Bank House.

INVERNESS, N.B., Convent of the Immaculate Conception.

LONDON, Notting Hill, W., Convent, Portoello Road; boarding-school for young ladies and lady boarders. Attached to the Convent is St. Elizabeth's Home, opened 4th October 1868, for the training of young girls as domestic servants.

MILL HILL, London, N.W., St. Mary's Franciscan Convent. These Religious are of the Third Order Regular of St. Francis, with the Rule and Constitutions of the other Franciscan houses in London and Scotland, confirmed to them by Papal Rescript of his Holiness Pius IX. The Divine Office, according to the Franciscan Breviary, is recited daily for all benefactors. They have charge of St. Margaret's Industrial School. They also take a limited number of young ladies to board in St. George's School, and day-boarders, and have a village school, St. Michael's, which is chiefly attended by the Protestant children of the neighbourhood. The Sisters are trained for home and foreign mission-work.

TAUNTON, Somerset, Convent of Our Lady of Dolours. This Community was founded in 1621 at Brussels, by the Rev. Father John Gennings, O.S.F., who had restored in England the English Province of the Friars of the Observance. From Brussels the Nuns removed to Nieuport in 1637, then to Bruges in 1662. At the French Revolution, 1792, they crossed v·· to England, fixing their abode first at the Abbey House, Winchester, and lastly at Taunton in 1808. They keep enclosure, recite the Divine Office in choir, and after a year's novitiate make perpetual vows. They devote themselves to the education of a small number of young ladies of the higher classes. They have also a middle school for training servants and for destitute children.

WOODCHESTER, Gloucestershire, Convent of the Immaculate Conception (August 1860), a filiation of Taunton; Orphanage for girls and an Institute for young women.

DRUMSHAMBO, Carrick-on-Shannon, Co. Leitrim, Convent of Perpetual Adoration (St. Mary of the Angels). This branch of the Third Order of St. Francis, called of "Strict Observance," is of French origin. The Institute takes its rise from the great reform of Picpus, A.D.

1613, when particular constitutions were approved and confirmed for it by Urban VIII. The Community is enclosed and contemplative. The objects of their life are praise and reparation to the Sacrament of the Altar by means of the perpetual adoration and exposition of the Blessed Sacrament both day and night, and prayer and penance for the conversion of sinners.

Habit.—Gray woollen, with cord and sandals; the figure of a monstrance is worked on the scapular and cloak.

This is the only house of this branch in the United Kingdom.

Good Shepherd (Nuns of the).

A branch of Our Lady of Charity of Refuge, and founded in 1835 by Mother Mary of St. Euphrasia Pelletier, Prioress of the Refuge at Angers, which, with several other Convents, was authorised by Pope Gregory XVI. to form themselves into a separate Congregation under the name of Our Lady of Charity of the Good Shepherd, and to elect a Superioress-General, to whom their future foundations should be subject.

Object.—The reclamation and instruction of women and girls who have fallen, or are in danger of falling, the perfectly reformed among whom are ultimately suitably provided and cared for.

Rule.—Enclosure; the vows of poverty, chastity, and obedience, and a fourth vow to labour for the salvation of erring souls, are taken after two years' novitiate.

Habit.—White serge, with scapular, blue cord or cincture, and black veil. On breast a silver heart, with the Blessed Virgin and Child; and on the reverse the figure of the Good Shepherd.

The first house in England was founded at Hammersmith in 1841. From it have since been founded the houses mentioned below.

The Convent at Finchley is the Provincial House and Novitiate for the Order in Great Britain.

ENGLISH PROVINCE:

BRISTOL, Convent, Arno's Vale (22nd July 1851); certified reformatory school for girls (1866); house of refuge for penitents (1861). A cemetery attached.

CARDIFF, Glamorganshire, Convent, with house for penitents.

FINCHLEY, Middlesex, Convent, East End, with a house for penitent female prisoners.

GLASGOW, N.B., Convent, Dalbeth House; certified reformatory school for girls and Magdalen asylum.

LIVERPOOL, Convent, Ford; house of refuge for female penitents (1858).

LONDON, Hammersmith, W.; house of refuge for penitents.

MANCHESTER, Convent, Blackley; house of refuge for penitents.

IRISH PROVINCE:

BALYNAFEIGH, Belfast, industrial Magdalen penitentiary, wholly dependent on proceeds of laundry.

CORK, Sunday's Well, Magdalen asylum and certified industrial school.

LIMERICK, Magdalen asylum for 100 penitents, and certified industrial and reformatory schools.

NEW ROSS, Co. Wexford, middle-class and certified industrial school.

WATERFORD, 1, Convent, with Magdalen asylum for penitents; 2, Convent, with certified industrial school.

Helpers of the Holy Souls.

Founded at Paris in December 1856, by Mademoiselle Eugénie Smet. The Congregation received the approbation of Pius IX. in 1869 and again in 1873; finally was fully approved of by Leo XIII. in 1878.

With the approbation of his Eminence Cardinal Manning, the Society was introduced into England in 1873.

Object.—In the words of the motto of the Congregation, " To pray, suffer, and labour for the souls in purgatory;" they devote themselves to all the works of mercy, especially home and foreign missions, and visiting the sick and poor in their own homes. In connection with the Congregation are two classes of persons living in the world, "Lady Associates" and "Honorary Members."

Rule of St. Ignatius. Vows of poverty, chastity, and obedience; and offering of all their works for the souls in purgatory. The Congregation is divided into choir Nuns and lay Sisters.

LONDON, 1, Gloucester Road, Regent's Park, N.W.

JERSEY, St. Heliers, Beaulieu, St. Saviour's Road.

Holy Child Jesus (Sisters of).

Founded within the last few years. Mother House at St. Leonards-on-Sea.

Object.—Education of rich and poor.

BLACKPOOL, Lancashire, Convent of SS. Hearts of Jesus and Mary, Layton Hill (branch from house at St. Leonards-on-Sea); boarding-school for young ladies; Poor Schools of Sacred Hearts of Jesus and Mary.

EDGBASTON, Birmingham, Convent, 59 Hagley Road.

HURST GREEN, Sussex, Convent at May-

SISTERS OF THE HOLY CROSS.

field. Preparatory school in connection with establishment at St. Leonards-on-Sea.

LONDON, Convent, 12 and 13 Nottingham Place, W. (from St. Leonards-on-Sea); for the education of young ladies, who are received as boarders, weekly and day boarders, and general day-pupils.

PRESTON, Lancashire, Convent, 22 Winckley Square; school for young ladies at the Convent, and also a junior school for little boys and girls under nine; and the Government schools of the English Martyrs, St. Ignatius, St. Walburge, and St. Wilfrid. Most of the teachers of these schools board in the Convent.

ST. LEONARDS-ON-SEA, Sussex, Convent of All Souls (Mother House), with church (for inmates only) of St. Michael (Oct. 1868); first and second class boarding-schools for young ladies.

TUNBRIDGE WELLS, Convent, Mark Cross; boarding-school. Fine Gothic structure by W. Pugin, erected and partially endowed by the late Dowager Duchess of Leeds, 1866. A limited number of orphans of middle class are received on the endowment.

Holy Cross and Passion, Sisters of the Most.

Founded in 1851 at Manchester, by Father Gaudentius, of St. Stephen, Passionist, and the Very Rev. Provost Croskell, V.G.

SISTERS OF THE HOLY FAITH.

Objects.—A Home for factory girls, instruction of the poor and middle classes, visitation of the sick, &c.

BATLEY CARR; Poor Schools.

BOLTON, Lancashire, Mount St. Joseph, Dean; Convents, 42 Clarence Street and 28 Pilkington Street; in charge of public elementary schools for girls of St. Edmund, St. Marie, St. Patrick, and SS. Peter and Paul.

DEWSBURY; Poor School for girls.

HUDDERSFIELD; Poor Schools.

MANCHESTER, Convent, 31 Byrom Street; in charge of St. Mary's public elementary school.

SALFORD; public elementary school of St. Peter.

SUTTON, Lancashire;Poor S chools.

KILCULLEN, Co. Kildare.

Holy Faith, Sisters of the.

GLASNEVIN. Superioress, Mrs. Aylward. Boarding-school for young ladies; boarders, fifty; two Poor Schools, one for girls and one for little boys; poor children, 150.

St. Brigid's Orphanage, 46 Eccles Street, Dublin. This institution was established under the patronage of the late Cardinal Cullen, in 1857, to protect Catholic orphans and destitute children in danger of loss of faith

1740 orphans (boys and girls) have been already admitted; more than 1500 have been reared, educated, and put to trades or placed in situations; and about 200 are at present in the institution. The orphanage is supported entirely by voluntary contributions.

Clarendon St. (19 to 22), three large Poor Schools, one for girls, one for little boys, and one for infants; seven hundred children.

Convent of the Holy Faith, 23 Clarendon Street; day-school for young ladies.

Jervis Street (65 Lower), House of the Society of the B.V.M. " Queen of Charity;" two Poor Schools, one for girls and one for little boys; four hundred children. The poorest receive breakfast daily. The large Poor Schools, Park Street, West Coombe, are attended by Sisters from this house; five hundred children, two hundred of whom receive breakfast daily, and clothing when funds permit.

Dominick Street (54 Lower), "Our Lady of the Rosary;" day-school for young ladies, and a junior class for little boys.

SKERRIES, County Dublin; schools of the "Sacred Heart;" two pension schools, one for girls and one for little boys.

CELBRIDGE, Co. Kildare; three Poor Schools, one for girls, one for little boys, and one for infants; three hundred children; one pension school at the Convent.

MULLINAVATT, Co. Kilkenny, Mount St. Joseph;" two Poor Schools, one for girls and one for little boys, and a pension school.

The schools of the Holy Faith are not connected with the National Board.

Holy Sepulchre, Canonesses of the.

Corresponding Order to the Canons of the Holy Sepulchre, who trace their origin to the Apostle St. James the Just, the first Bishop of Jerusalem, by whom priests were appointed to watch over the Holy Places. These built a temple close to the Holy Sepulchre, over which, after two centuries of desecration by the Romans, a church was erected by St. Helena, mother of the Emperor Constantine, in laying the foundation of which the true Cross was discovered. Religious houses were subsequently established both for women and men. The Canonesses, who claim to be coeval with the Canons, and reckon St. Mary Magdalen, St. Martha, and St. Helena among the members of their Order, withdrew, as well as the Canons, from Jerusalem on its occupation by the Turks in 1287. In August 1794 an English branch of the Order, which had been founded at Liége by Miss Susanna Hawley in 1642, came over to England in consequence of the French Revolution. After a residence at Holme, in Yorkshire, and at Dean House, near Salisbury, they purchased, in March 1800, their present abode, with fifty-eight acres

of land, at New Hall, near Chelmsford, formerly
a palace (of which but one side remains) of
Mary, and occasionally of Elizabeth, Queens of
England. The Canonesses have since devoted
themselves to the education of young ladies,
whom they receive as boarders.

Rule.—Of St. Augustine, with additional
constitutions, approved by Urban VIII., uniting
the active with the contemplative. Observance
of canonical hours, rising at four A.M., &c.;
yearly renewal of vows; annual retreats. Prioress elected for life, under jurisdiction of Bishop
of the diocese, there being no Generalate of the
Order. Recital of the Divine Office is their
special object. Enclosed.

Habit.—Black serge, under white rochet,
without sleeves; on left side a double red cross;
in choir a long black cloak, likewise with a
double red cross, and a red cord and tassels.
The Canonesses wear a gold ring with a double
cross.

CHELMSFORD, Essex, Convent at New Hall;
boarding-school for the higher education of
young ladies.

Hope, Sisters of (or Sœurs de l'Esperance).

For nursing invalids, of whatever creed,
at their homes. These are a branch or Congregation of the Society of the Holy Family,
founded at Bordeaux in 1820 by the Abbé

Noailles, and designed by its founder to undertake all kinds of good works. Each Congregation, of which there are seven, has its special mission and Novitiate; those in England are the Sisters of Hope and the Sisters of the Immaculate Conception.

The Society is governed by a priest, who is called the Director-General. He is assisted by a Pro-Director-General, by the Directress-General, and her assistants. The general house is at Bordeaux. This house is the residence of the Directress-General, her assistants, and the Superior-General of each branch of the association.

By a decree of the Congregation of Bishops and Regulars, dated the 5th September 1843, the Holy Father praised and recommended this association in the most solemn manner.

LONDON, Kilburn, N.W., Convent, Hope House, Quex Road.

Immaculate Conception (Sisters of the).

A Congregation of the Holy Family, for the higher branches of education, schools for the middle classes, Poor Schools, and all works of charity. The Novitiate is at Rockferry, near Liverpool.

HARROGATE ; boarding-school for young ladies.

LEEDS ; Convent of Immaculate Conception; St. Mary's Orphanage, for girls; schools for girls and infants; founded 1852.

LEITH, N.B.; Poor Schools.

LISCARD, Birkenhead.

LONDON, Convent of St. Mary's, 16 Great Prescot Street, Goodman's Fields, E.

MACCLESFIELD, Cheshire.

SICKLINGHALL; Poor Schools.

STALYBRIDGE, Cheshire.

STOCKPORT, Cheshire, Convent, St. Joseph's, Petersgate.

WREXHAM, Denbigh.

NEWBRIDGE, Co. Kildare, Convent, St. Conleith's Abbey; higher and middle-class schools; Poor Schools; visiting the poor and sick, &c.

- **Institute of Charity (Sisters of Providence of the).**

Founded by the Abbate Rosmini, in connection with his Institute for men, assisted by Giovanna Antonietti, for the education of children in country districts, where the priests are unable to bear the expenses of a regular Convent, for which purpose three or more Sisters are sent out from the Central House, returning to it at the end of evry scholastic year. Approved and sanctioned by Gregory XVI. in 1839. Introduced into England, at Loughborough, by Lady Arundell of Wardour in 1843, which is the Central House for this country.

CARDIFF, Glamorganshire; poor and middle-class schools, and instruction for women and girls.

LONDON, Holborn, E.C., Convent, 15 Ely Place (next to St. Etheldreda's Church); day-school for young ladies, Poor Schools, and instruction for women and girls.

LOUGHBOROUGH, Leicestershire, Central House; boarding-school for young ladies; spiritual retreats for ladies; Poor Schools; instruction of women and girls. It is proposed at an early date to establish here the Perpetual Adoration of the Blessed Sacrament, in addition to the other works.

RUGBY, Warwickshire; Poor Schools; instruction for women and girls.

Institute of the Blessed Virgin Mary.

Originally a Congregation founded by Mary Ward in the seventeenth century, and suppressed by the Holy See. Reconstructed after her death, and approved by Clement XI. in 1703, and finally approved in 1877 by Pius IX. In Germany the Institute is known by the name of the "English Virgins" or "English Ladies." Two distinct Congregations, each governed by a Generaless, exist, one with its head-quarters in Austria, the other in Bavaria.

The English houses of York and Hammersmith were founded towards the close of the seventeenth century by Frances Bedingfield, a daughter of Francis Bedingfield, Esq., of Bedingfield, Suffolk. These houses were for a hundred years the only Convents in England for the education of the daughters of the Catholic nobility and gentry. The Irish branch of the Institute, having the Convent at Rathfarnham, near Dublin, for its Mother House, sprang from York—the foundress, Mary Teresa Ball, having made her novitiate there—and from it in turn at least fifty houses have come into existence. Besides its numerous communities in Ireland, where they are best known as Loreto Nuns, the Mother House at Rathfarnham has houses depending on it in America, India, and many of the colonies and dependencies of the British Crown.

ASCOT, Berks, founded from Haverstock Hill.

LEEK, Staffordshire.

LONDON, Haverstock Hill, N.W., Convent of St. Mary, Gifford Lodge, England Lane, founded from Nymphenburg, Bavaria.

MANCHESTER, Hulme, Convent of Our Lady of Loreto, Upper Moss Lane, founded from Rathfarnham. Boarding-school for young ladies; high-school for day-pupils; four large elementary schools.

INSTITUTE OF B. VIRGIN MARY.

YORK, Convent of St. Mary (1680), Micklegate Bar; boarding-school for young ladies; middle-class school; Poor Schools. The oldest existing Convent in England.

BALBRIGGAN, Co. Dublin.

BRAY, Co. Wicklow (1850); boarding-school and Poor Schools.

CLONMEL, Tipperary, Convent of St. Joseph of the Isle; day-school for the upper and middle classes.

DALKEY, Co. Dublin.

DUBLIN:
- North Great George's Street, 43 and 44 (founded 1837); boarding and day schools.
- Stephen's Green East, 53; boarding and day schools; Poor Schools.
- Kenilworth Square; day-school.

ENNISCORTHY, Co. Wexford; day-school for young ladies.

FERMOY, Co. Cork.

GOREY, Co. Wexford; boarding-school; middle-class day-school; national school.

KILKENNY.

KILLARNEY, Co. Kerry.

LETTERKENNY, Co. Donegal.

NAVAN, Co. Meath; first-class boarding-school for young ladies.

OMAGH, Co. Tyrone.

RATHFARNHAM, Co. Dublin, Loreto Abbey (the Mother House in Ireland, 1822); boarding, day, and poor schools.

TOX VIEW, Killarney.

WEXFORD, Richmond House; ladies' school.

YOUGHAL, Clifton, Co. Cork, Convent of St. Anne. Ladies desirous of leading a retired life received as parlour boarders. Large day, primary, and Sunday schools.

John of God, Sisters of St.

Founded in 1871 at Wexford, by the Most Rev. Dr. Furlong, Bishop of Ferns, in affiliation to the Order of St. John of God in Rome.

Object.—Care of the sick of all classes, at home and in hospital. Also take charge of industrial schools, and of works appróved by the Bishop.

Rule of St. Augustine. Vows of poverty, chastity, and obedience, and devotion to the sick poor, after two and a half years novitiate.

CARRICK-ON-SUIR, Co. Tipperary.

CASTLECOMER, Co. Kilkenny; Workhouse Hospital.

KILMACTHOMAS, Co. Waterford.

NEW ROSS, Co. Wexford.

WEXFORD, Sallyville, Mother House. In

charge of workhouse hospital; home for aged men and women; Poor School. (The Sisters reside in the workhouse hospitals at the above places.)

Joseph, Sisters of St.

Founded in 1650 in Le Puy-en-Velay, by the Bishop of Le Puy, Monseigneur de Maupas; Mother House at Clermont. Introduced into England, at Devizes, within the last few years.

Objects.—The education of all classes, visitation of the sick and poor, care of hospitals and orphanages, and works of charity in general.

Rule of St. Ignatius.

ABERSYCHAN, Monmouthshire.

DEVIZES, Wilts, Convent, St. Joseph's Place.

MALMESBURY, Wilts.

NEWPORT, Monmouthshire, Convent, Arundel House; principal house and Novitiate; boarding-school for young ladies; Poor Schools.

WESTBURY-ON-TRYM, Convent of St. Joseph.

St. Joseph de Cluni, Sisters of St.

This Congregation, founded in 1806 by the Rev. Mother Anne Mary Javouhey, has for its first object the sanctification of its own members, by means of the Religious and Community life, and afterwards the exercise of works of zeal and charity, as much for the care of the sick and the poor as for the instruction of youth.

The Institute is composed of choir and lay Sisters, who make equally the three simple vows of religion—first for a time, and afterwards perpetual. Confirmed by the Holy See in 1854.

Habit.—The choir Sisters wear a pelerine and black veil, a blue woollen gown, a large scapular of black serge, a rosary with crucifix hanging at the left side; also a crucifix suspened on the bosom by a blue cord, and a ring on the third finger of the left hand.

The lay Sisters wear a blue robe of the same stuff, a black apron and shawl, a white cornet with small black veil, a crucifix suspended from the neck with a black cord, and the profession ring on the left hand.

Little Company of Mary.

Nursing Sisters.

NOTTINGHAM, Hyson Green.

QUORNDON, Leicestershire.

Little Sisters of the Poor.

Founded in 1840 at St. Servan, in Brittany, by Abbé Le Pailleur, the Curé, with the assistance of two young working women, Marie Augustine (now Mother Superior-General) and Marie Thérèse; joined afterwards by a servant named Jeanne Jugan, and another woman, Fanchon Aubert. Approved by Pius IX. in 1854.

Object.—The care of aged people of both sexes, irrespective of creed.

The Little Sisters of the Poor have no funds or income whatever. They support their aged inmates by whatever public charity affords them, collecting daily, from house to house, scraps of food, old clothing, alms in money, or anything that may be offered to them. The institution is a Catholic one, but no distinction is made for admission. Provided the applicants are destitute but respectable old people, incapable of gaining their own livelihood, and have no person to gain it for them, they are fit objects for the house of the Little Sisters of the Poor.

The Little Sisters have now more than two hundred and forty houses, containing many thousands of poor, who have thus found a comfortable home for their declining years. Mother House at Rennes.

BIRKENHEAD, Cheshire, Parkfield Avenue.

BRIGHTON, Sussex, 22 Wellington Road.

BRISTOL, Cotham Park, Cotham Hill; House of Refuge for aged poor.

CARLISLE, Cumberland, Convent, Milbourne Street (1880).

EDINBURGH, N.B., Convent, 43 Gilmore Place.

GLASGOW, N.B., Convent, 180 Garngad Hill; Asylum for aged poor.

GREENOCK, N.B., Convent, 46 Union Street.

HARBORNE, near Birmingham; Asylum for aged poor, St. Joseph's Home.

LEEDS, Convent of St. Joseph, Belle Vue Road (1865); Asylum for aged poor.

LIVERPOOL:
    Belmont Grove, Aigburth Road.
    Belmont Road, St. Joseph's Home.
    Hope Street.

LOCHEE, N.B., Convent, Wellburn.

LONDON:
    Notting Hill, W., Convent, St. Joseph's House, Portobello Road; Asylum for aged poor.
    South Lambeth, S.W., Convent, St. Peter's House, Meadow Road.
    Stoke Newington, N., Manor Road.

MANCHESTER:
    Plymouth Grove, 201; Asylum for aged and infirm poor.
    Culcheth Lane, Newton Heath; Asylum for aged poor.

NEWCASTLE-ON-TYNE, Northumberland, Convent, Meadow Bank, Elswick, 1886.

PRESTON, Lancashire, Springfield, Broughton Road; Home for aged poor.

PLYMOUTH, Hartley, St. Joseph's Home.

SHEFFIELD, Shrewsbury Road.

SUNDERLAND, High Barnes, Chester Road.

CORK, Convent, Montenotte.

DUBLIN, 121 Lower Coombe; Home for aged.

LISMORE, Co. Waterford.

Louis, Sisters of St.

Founded by the Abbé Bautin, Vicar-General, at Juilly, near Paris, in 1841; rules approved by Gregory XVI., 17th July 1844; founded at Lake View, Monaghan, Ireland, in 1859.

Rule of St. Augustine.
Habit.—Black.

ARTHURSTOWN, Convent, Ramsgrange; boarding and day schools for young ladies; Poor Schools.

BUNDORAN, Co. Donegal; boarding and day school; Poor School.

MIDDLETOWN, Co. Armagh; boarding-school for young ladies, who are prepared for the Civil Service intermediate examinations; Poor School; Orphanage.

MONAGHAN, Convent, Lakeview; first-class boarding-school. The Sisters of St. Louis also manage an Orphanage and Reformatory School, both separate and distinct institutions, besides a large Poor School for the children of the town and neighbourhood.

Little Schools (Sisters of the).

A French educational Community.

GUERNSEY, St. Mary's.

Marie Auxiliatrice, Sisters of.

The Religious of Marie Auxiliatrice devote themselves to the education of young ladies whom they receive as boarders, and also as day-boarders.

Daily Exposition and Benediction of the most Blessed Sacrament.

NOTTING HILL, London, W., Convent, The Lodge, St. James's Square (branch of house in Paris, 28 Rue du Maubeuge); boarding and day school for young ladies, middle-class school, and (at 10 St. Anne's Villas) school for little boys; lady boarders.

Marie Reparatrice, Sisters of.

Founded in France in 1857 by a noble Belgian lady out of devotion to the Immaculate Conception. Approved by Pius IX., and finally by Leo XIII., 18th April 1883.

Objects.—Daily and nightly adoration of the Blessed Sacrament, spiritual retreats and religious instruction for women of all classes, foreign missions, and, as far as possible, all works of a spiritually *reparative* or restorative character. . In a great measure supported by needlework and the contributions of the faithful. Are divided into choir Nuns and *coadjutrix* Sisters, and are governed by a Mother-Superior-General, resident at Rome.

Rule of St. Ignatius, with suitable modifications.

Habit.—White and blue for choir Nuns, and black for *coadjutrix* Sisters.

LONDON, Convent, Harley House, Brunswick Place, Marylebone Row, N.W. (January 1863); Exposition of the Blessed Sacrament from 7.30 A.M. until Benediction at 5.15 P.M.

LIMERICK, Laurel Hill Avenue, Convent of Marie Réparatrice.

Marist Nuns.

Founded in 1823, in the diocese of Belley, Ain, France, by the Very Rev. Père Colin (who instituted the Marist Fathers), for the education of female youth. Mother House at Belley, Ain, France.

Rule of St. Augustine.

LONDON:

Peckham, S.E., Convent, 60 Queen's Road; middle-class and Poor School.

Spitalfields, E., Convent of St. Anne.

Albert Place, Spicer Street, E.; middle-class schools; Poor Schools; Orphanage.

RICHMOND, Surrey, Convent, Grove Lodge, Queen's Road; higher-class boarding-school for young ladies.

CARRICK-ON-SHANNON, Co. Leitrim; boarding, middle-class, and Poor Schools.

Mercy, Sisters of.

Founded 12th Dec. 1831 by Catherine McAuley, in Lower Baggot Street, Dublin, where that lady had previously, 24th Sept. 1827, opened an institution for the education of poor girls and the reception of female orphans and destitute young women. Introduced into England, at Bermondsey, in Nov. 1839, by the foundress herself, and carried on by Miss Agnew and Miss Taylor, who had been previously prepared in the Convent of Mercy at Cork. Approved by the Holy See, 5th July 1841.

Objects.—All works of mercy, corporal and spiritual, especially education; the visiting of the sick poor at home and in hospital; the reception of destitute young women into a House of Mercy (which, as well as Poor Schools for girls, &c., must be attached, if possible, to every Convent), &c.

Rule of the Presentation Order, suitably adapted. No Generalate. Each Convent has its own Mother-Superior; but all the houses are subject to one rule.

The Sisters generally remain in the same Convent, or are changed about where there are branch houses. Each Convent is subject to the Bishop of the diocese and its own Mother-Superior.

Habit of black serge; veil, black, of thinner material; white coif and guimpe. Church, cloaks of white serge.

Novitiate, two years, preceded by six months' probation as postulants.

Vows are of "poverty, chastity, obedience, and the service of the poor, sick, and ignorant; and to persevere until death in the Congregation of our Blessed Lady of Mercy."

ABINGDON, Berks, Convent of Our Lady of Mercy, Oxford Road; boarding-school for young ladies; preparatory school for young gentlemen from three to nine years of age; founded in 1860.

ALDERNEY, St. Anne's Convent. Was opened as a branch house from the Convent of Mercy in Guernsey on July 15th, 1874. It was made a separate foundation on October 15th, 1881.

The Sisters are devoted to the works of mercy for the poor, sick, and ignorant of the island.

ALDERSHOT (branch from Abingdon); Poor and superior day schools.

ALTON, Stoke-on-Trent, Convent of St. John Baptist; boarding-school for young ladies; Poor Schools.

BEVERLEY; boarding-school for young ladies; Poor School.

BIRMINGHAM, St. Anne's, The Ravenhurst, Camphill, founded from Wandsworth. The works carried on by this Community at present are district schools at St. Anne's, Alcester Street; St. Catherine's, Horse Fair; the Oratory schools, Hyde Road. Attached to the Convent there are a middle-class boarding-school, and a day-school for girls and younger boys. The Sisters visit the sick poor, instruct adults, and give shelter to a limited number of young girls, whom they train as servants.

They relieve the poor at the Convent as far as means will permit.

BLACKBROOK, St. Helen's (branch from Mount Vernon). The Sisters have charge of the schools—boys, girls, and infants—containing over three hundred children. It is also a home for the pupil-teachers and a few boarders.

BRENTWOOD, Essex; boarding-school for young ladies; Poor School; Orphanage for girls.

BRIDGWATER; schools; visit of sick.

BRIGHTON, Bristol Road, St. Joseph's. This

Community was founded from Bermondsey on June 11th, 1852.

The Sisters take charge of the girl and infant schools of the parish of St. John the Baptist, instruct adults, and relieve as well as visit the sick and poor.

Attached to the Convent are: (1) an Orphanage (the buildings are capable of accommodating fifty girls); (2) a Home of Preservation, supported by St. Elizabeth's Society; (3) a laundry, in which women and girls of good character are employed.

During the winter and early spring, benefactors provide the Convent with means for giving dinners on four days of the week.

BRISTOL, Dighton Street.

BURNLEY, Lancashire, St. Mary's Schools.

CARLTON, Notts, Orphanage; elementary school; branch from Derby.

CARLTON, Selby; branch from Clifford; Poor Schools.

CLECKHEATON, Yorkshire, St. Gregory's Convent; instruction of children; visit of the sick. The Convent, a handsome building, with large chapel, was raised by the efforts of the Benedictine Fathers and the generosity of two friends in 1885.

CLIFFORD, Tadcaster (founded from Bermondsey); Poor School; visit of the sick.

COVENTRY, Gosford Green, St. Joseph's boarding-school for young ladies; Poor School; lady boarders.

DERBY, Convent of St. Joseph; elementary and middle-class school; visit of the sick.

DORNIE, Kintail, N.B.

DOUGLAS, Isle of Man, elementary school.

DUNDEE, N.B., St. Joseph's Poor School.

EDINBURGH, Lauriston Gardens, St. Catherine's Convent of Mercy. Founded in Edinburgh in 1858 by a Scotch lady (Miss Helen Margaret Grant), who was its first Superior. The present Convent was built for the Community through the munificence of the late Mrs. Hutchison, and was opened in 1861.

The House of Mercy was opened in 1880. This institution owes its existence mainly to the zeal and charity of the Dowager Duchess of Buccleuch, and is under her immediate patronage. The Sisters teach the greater number of the Edinburgh as well as the Dalkeith and Slateford Catholic Poor Schools, and also a boarding-school within the Convent grounds, in which, in addition to the ordinary branches of a high-class English education, the pupils are taught languages and various accomplishments.

ELGIN, N.B.; Poor School.

ELTHAM, Co. Kent, Convent of St. Mary;

certified Industrial school for girls and Orphanage, Torrington Lodge. Branch from Bermondsey (about to be removed to West Croydon, Surrey).

GAINSBOROUGH, Lincolnshire; boarding-school for girls.

GLASGOW, N.B., Convent, Hill Street, Garnet Hill; Home for servants out of place; Poor School.

GRAVESEND, Kent; Poor Schools (founded from Bermondsey).

GUERNSEY; middle-class boarding-school; girls' Poor School; infant school.

HANDSWORTH, Birmingham, Convent of St. Mary; boarding-school; Poor School; House of Mercy.

HEXHAM, Northumberland, Convent of St. Mary; Poor School.

HULL, Convent, Anlaby Road; Poor School.

KEITH, N.B., Poor School.

LANCASTER, Convent of St. Walburga; elementary school (branch from Mount Vernon, Liverpool).

LEEDS, Hunslet, St. Joseph's middle-class school.

LIVERPOOL:

Convent of St. Ethelburga, Mount Vernon, E.; House of Mercy; large Poor Schools.

Founded in 1843 by four Sisters from Baggot Street, Dublin, the parent house of the Sisters of Mercy. The Sisters are devoted to a threefold work of charity : (1) the protection of women of good character; (2) the visitation of the sick ; and (3) the education of poor children.

Convent of St. Elizabeth, 64 Breckfield Road South; certified Industrial school for girls; Institute and Asylum for training girls as servants (branch from Mount Vernon).

Convent of St. Vincent, 24 Hardy Street; schools (branch from Mount Vernon).

LONDON :

Bermondsey, S.E., Convent of our Lady of Mercy; Poor Schools ; middle-class school; visitation of the sick; and instruction of adults, &c. Certified Industrial school and Orphanage at Eltham or West Croydon. Founded 1839 by the Rev. Peter Butler, assisted by the Baroness Montesquieu and Lady Barbara Eyre, and established by Mother McAuley herself, the foundress of the Institute of Mercy.

Blandford Square, 47, N.W., Convent of St. Edward; House of Mercy; Orphanage; Home for servants.

Chelsea, S.W., Convent of St. Joseph, Cadogan Street (founded from Bermondsey); boarding-school for young ladies ; middle-class day-school; Poor Schools; visit the sick and instruct adults.

Commercial Road East, 535, E., Poor Schools.

Crispin Street, 50 (Bishopsgate Street Without), E., Poor Schools ; Providence Night Refuge for homeless men, women, and children.

Ormond Street, Great, 46, W.C., Hospital of St. John of Jerusalem and St. Elizabeth, for female patients suffering from advanced incurable disease, or requiring long medical treatment and careful nursing.

MANSFIELD, Nottingham.

MARYVALE, Perry Barr, Birmingham, Convent of St. Mary; built by Pugin ; Poor School; middle school ; House of Mercy.

MIDDLESBROUGH, King's Road, North Ormesby.

NEWCASTLE-ON-TYNE, Westgate Road (from Mount Vernon, Liverpool), founded in 1855 by Miss Dunn; Poor and middle-class schools ; House of Mercy.

NORTH SHIELDS, Northumberland ; Poor Schools (St. Cuthbert's).

NOTTINGHAM, Convent of our Blessed Lady; middle-class boarding-school ; House of Mercy for servants; Convent of St. John ; Orphanage for girls.

OLDHAM, Lancashire ; girls' and infant schools, St. Mary's and St. Patrick's ; Home for the training of pupil-teachers; middle-class boarding-school.

OLD SWAN, Liverpool; elementary school (St. Oswald's) (branch from Mount Vernon).

ROCHDALE (branch from Oldham).

RYDE, Isle of Wight; boarding-school; Poor School.

SHEFFIELD, St. Catherine's; Poor Schools.

SHREWSBURY, Poor School.

STUDLEY, Redditch, St. Mary's Poor Schools; visit of the sick.

SUNDERLAND, Monkwearmouth, Durham; Poor Schools (St. Mary's and St. Benet's).

TOMINTOUL, Banffshire, N.B.

TOW LAW, Darlington, Cumberland; Poor School.

WALTHAMSTOW, Essex, Convent, Walthamstow House; Poor School, certified by Government.

WHITBY, boarding-school for young ladies.

WIGTON, Cumberland; Poor School (St. Cuthbert's).

WOLVERHAMPTON, Convent of St. Joseph, founded in January, 1849. The works of the Community comprise—elementary schools in the four districts of the town; middle-class boarding and day schools; House of Mercy for the protection and training of young women of good character only; the visitation of the sick and relief of the poor; evening classes for adults.

ABBEYFEALE, Co. Limerick, founded 1871, on site of old Cistercian Abbey; schools under National Board; visit of the sick.

ADARE, Co. Limerick; founded in 1854 by Lord Dunraven on site of old Trinitarian Abbey; schools; visit of the sick.

ARDEE, Co. Louth; day-school for young ladies; Workhouse Hospital.

ARKLOW, Co. Wicklow; school for middle and higher classes; national school.

ATHLONE, free school; Summer Hill female Industrial schools.

ATHY, Co. Kildare; day-school for the middle class; school in connection with the National Board of Education; novices trained for the Australian mission; charge of the Workhouse Hospital; House of Mercy for training domestic servants. An office for extern servants is also attached.

BALLINAMORE, Carrick-on-Shannon, Co. Leitrim.

BALLINASLOE, Convent of St. Gabriel; schools.

BALLINROBE, Claremorris, Co. Mayo; national schools.

BALLYMAHON, Mullingar.

BALLYSHANNON, Co. Donegal, Convent of St. Catherine (opened 30th April 1867).

BANTRY, Co. Cork, founded 1860. Convent erected by Miss Murphy of Cork; four large schools and other works of mercy.

BELFAST, Co. Antrim, St. Paul's Convent, Crumlin Road, founded 1854. First Convent opened in Belfast. Large national schools; better class day-school. An Orphanage and Industrial school for one hundred and fifty. In connection with this Convent, the Mater Infirmorum Hospital, under the care of the Sisters, was opened November 1st, 1883, for the relief of the sick and dying poor without distinction of creed.

Convent of Our Lady of Mercy, Sussex Place; built in 1879, and is a branch of the Convent of Our Lady of Mercy, Crumlin Road. Attached to the Convent are St. Malachy's national schools, and a school for the better class.

BELTURBET, Co. Cavan.

BIRR, King's Co.; school for young ladies; Industrial school; primary Poor School.

BORRIS-IN-OSSORY, Queen's Co.

BORRISOLEIGH, Co. Tipperary (branch from Templemore).

BOYLE, Co. Roscommon.

CAHIR, Co. Tipperary, Convent, New Inn.

CALLAN, Co. Kilkenny.

CAPPOQUIN, Co. Waterford, Convent of Our Lady of Mercy; Poor and middle schools, and Industrial school for boys.

CARDONAGH, Co. Donegal (founded 1859); schools under National Board; visit of Workhouse, Hospital, and sick poor.

CARLOW.

CARRICK-ON-SUIR, Co. Tipperary (founded 1874); middle-class day-school; national school with over 200 pupils; charge of Workhouse Hospital.

CASTLERAR, Co. Mayo.

CASTLETOWN BEREHAVEN, Bantry, Co. Cork.

CHARLEVILLE, Co. Cork; Schools; Workhouse; visit of sick.

CLARA, King's Co.

CLAREMORRIS, County Mayo; large Poor Schools; visit of sick.

CLIFDEN, Co. Galway; Orphanage and Industrial school.

CLONAKILTY (founded 1856), House of Mercy; Orphanage; visit of Workhouse Hospital and sick; Industrial school for girls; day-schools.

COOTEHILL (founded 1881), one of the finest Convents in the country.

CORK:
Mercy Hospital; St. Marie of the Isles; Workhouse Hospital.

DOON, Pallasgreen, Co. Limerick; Poor Schools and Orphanage.

DOWNPATRICK, County Down, Mount St. Patrick's Schools; handsome Gothic Convent, connected with St. Patrick's Memorial Church.

DRANGAN, Callan.

DROGHEDA, St. Mary's.

DUBLIN:
Baggot Street, Lower, 64 (founded 1827), parent house of Community; girls trained to be schoolmistresses, others to be servants; school; Townsend national school.

Booterstown, Booterstown Avenue, Convent of St. Anne; school; Industrial school with 150 inmates.

Brickfield Lane, 2; St. Joseph's Night Refuge for homeless women and children (200 beds); supper served every evening to the homeless, and breakfast on Sunday and holy days; schools.

Gloster Street, Lower, 104, St. Mary's Penitent Retreat (founded 1822).

Golden Bridge, Convent of St. Vincent; St. Vincent Convict Refuge (1855); adult Reformatory; Poor Schools; Industrial schools with 90 girls.

Jervis Street Hospital and Convent (founded 1721).

Mater Misericordiæ Hospital, for 250 patients, Eccles Street.

South Dublin Union Hospital (614 beds).

DUNDALK, Co. Louth, Convent of St. Malachy (founded 1847); day-school for young ladies; national school; Sunday school for girls; new Orphanage, opened 24th August 1880; Industrial school; county Hospital; Workhouse; visit the sick and dying in their homes.

DUNGARVAN, Co. Waterford, Convent of Our Lady of Mercy; select school; national school; Workhouse and Infirmary.

DUNMORE, EAST, Co. Waterford (1863).

ELPHIN, Co. Roscommon.

ENNIS, Co. Clare; school for young ladies; primary Poor School.

ENNISCORTHY, Co. Wexford, Convent of Immaculate Conception; Poor School; visitation of sick.

ENNISKILLEN, Co. Fermanagh; large schools for the children of the town.

ENNISTIMON, County Clare; schools; Workhouse.

GALWAY; schools.
    Magdalen Asylum, College Road.
    Workhouse Hospital.

GORT, Co. Galway, Convent of St. Patrick (established 1857); free schools.

GRANARD, Co. Longford.

KANTURK, Co. Cork.

KELLS, Co. Meath.

KILCOCK, Co. Kildare.

KILKEE, Co. Clare; Orphanage.

KILKENNY; Workhouse Hospital.

KILLARNEY, Co. Kerry.

KILMACTHOMAS, Co. Waterford.

KILRUSH, Co. Clare; school for young ladies; Orphanage; primary Poor School; Union Hospital.

KINGSTOWN, Dublin, Refuge of St. Patrick, Crofton Road, for 100 female penitents (founded in Bow Street, 1798); Hospital of St. Michael.

KINSALE, Co. Cork (founded 1844).

KINVARA, Co. Galway; branch of Convent at Gort.

LIMERICK, Old Town, St. Mary's Refuge

for servants out of place; two schools with over 1600 pupils; female Confraternity of Holy Family and other sodalities.

LIMERICK, Mount St. Vincent Female Orphanage, with 250 children; two schools; Asylum for widows, founded and endowed by Rev. W. A. O'Meara, O.S.F.; general and fever Hospitals; female schools of Workhouse.

LONDONDERRY.

LONGFORD, St. Joseph's Convent; pupils prepared for intermediate examinations.

LOUGHREA, Co. Galway, Convent of St. Raphael; schools.

LURGAN, Co. Armagh; extensive schools.

MACROOM, Co. Cork; national schools; upper-class boarding-school; visit of sick.

MIDLETON; branch from Kinsale; the Sisters are matron and nurses at Workhouse.

MALLOW, Co. Cork.

MOATE, Co. Westmeath (founded 1861); certified Industrial school; national schools.

MOHILL, Cos. Leitrim and Longford.

MOVILLE, Co. Donegal.

NAAS, Co. Kildare.

NAVAN, Co. Meath.

NENAGH, Co. Tipperary; school for young ladies; primary and Poor Schools.

NEWCASTLE, WEST, Co. Limerick; schools.

NEW INN, Cahir, Tipperary.

NEW ROSS, Co. Wexford.

NEWRY, Co. Down, Convent of Sacred Heart; Home of Our Mother of Mercy for the aged poor, and destitute orphans Kilmorey Street, opened 24th September 1779.

NEWTOWN FORBES, Co. Longford, Convent of St. Michael; Industrial school.

OUGHTERARD, Co. Galway, Magdalen Asylum; Workhouse Hospital.

PARSONSTOWN or BIRR, King's Co.

PASSAGE WEST, Co. Cork.

PORTLAW, Co. Waterford.

PORTUMNA, Co. Galway, Convent of St. Joseph.

QUEENSTOWN, Co. Cork; national schools.

RATHDRUM, Co. Wicklow, Convent of St. Bridget; School of St. Mary for higher and middle classes; St. Michael's National School.

RATHKEALE, Co. Limerick; schools.

ROCHFORD BRIDGE, Killucan, Co. Westmeath.

ROSCOMMON; Industrial school for delicate

Catholic children; national schools; improved laundry.

ROSSTREVOR, Newry, Co. Down.

RUSHEEN, diocese of Tuam.

SKIBBEREEN, Co. Cork, Convent of the Immaculate Conception.

SLIGO; free school; Industrial and training schools for teachers.

STRABANE, Co. Tyrone; day-school; boarding-school; female Orphanage; certified Industrial school; pupils prepared for the intermediate examinations.

STRADBALLY, Co. Waterford; schools.

SWINEFORD, Co. Mayo; Workhouse.

TEMPLEMORE, Co. Tipperary; day-school for young ladies; Industrial school; Orphanage; national school.

THURLES, Co. Tipperary; Union.

TIPPERARY; Industrial school and Orphanage; Workhouse Hospital, Cashel.

TRALEE, Co. Kerry.

TRIM, Co. Meath.

TUAM, County Galway; national school; boarding-school; House of Mercy.

TULLAMORE, King's Co.

WATERFORD (branch from Kinsale); charge of Workhouse.

WESTPORT, Co. Mayo; Orphanage and Industrial school.

WEXFORD, Convent of St. Michael (founded 1840); House of Mercy; certified Industrial school; Orphanage for destitute children.

YOUGHAL (branch from Kinsale); charge of Workhouse.

Mercy, Our Lady of (Sisters of Charity of).

Founded in 1832 at Tilburg, in Holland, by Monseigneur Twysen, Archbishop of Utrecht.

Objects.—Education, especially of the poor; attendance on the sick and infirm, &c.

Rule of the founder.

NEWNHAM PADDOX, Co. Warwick, with Orphanage and Poor School.

PANTASAPH, Holywell, Co. Flint, Convent of St. Clare; boarding-school for young ladies of the middle class; Orphanage, devoted to the training of girls in the various branches of household work, and in plain sewing.

PRESTON, Lancashire, Convent of St. Joseph; Orphanage for girls, Theatre Street.

Misericorde (Sœurs de) de Séez.

Founded in 1823 at Séez, in Normandy, by M. Bazin, Vicar-General of the Diocesan Seminary.

Object.—The nursing of invalids of all

creeds and classes at their own homes. Supported by voluntary contributions of the sick, however small. Mother House at Séez.

LONDON, Hammersmith, W., St. Vincent's House, 49 Queen Street, for nursing invalids at home, rich or poor, Catholic or other.

Notre Dame, Sisters of (de Namur).

Founded in 1803 at Amiens, by Julie Billiart and the Viscountess Blin de Bourdon, under the auspices of the Bishop, Monseigneur de Villaret. Approved by Gregory XVI., 28th June 1844. Introduced into England at Penryn in 1845. Devoted to education in all its branches, from the most elementary to the highest, according to circumstances.

BIRKDALE PARK, Southport; boarding-school for young ladies; high school; parochial school.

BLACKBURN; boarding-school for young ladies; school for pupil-teachers; high school; parochial schools.

CLAPHAM (transferred from Penryn); boarding-school for young ladies; high school; parochial school.

LIVERPOOL:

Everton Valley; high school; school for pupil-teachers; parochial schools.

Falkner Street; girl's Orphanage.

Mount Pleasant; Training College for

schoolmistresses; school for pupil-teachers; high school; parochial schools.

LONDON:
Battersea; high school; school for pupil-teachers; parochial schools.
Brixton; high school.
Camberwell; high school; school for pupil-teachers; parochial school.
Islington; high school; parochial school.
St. George's; middle school; school for pupil-teachers; parochial schools.

MANCHESTER; high school; parochial schools.

NORTHAMPTON; boarding-school for young ladies; school for pupil-teachers; high school; parochial school.

NORWICH; boarding-school for young ladies; high school; parochial schools.

PLYMOUTH; boarding-school for young ladies; school for pupil-teachers; middle school; parochial schools.

SHEFFIELD; boarding-school for young ladies; high school; school for pupil-teachers; parochial schools.

ST. HELENS, near Liverpool; high school; school for pupil-teachers; parochial schools.

WARRINGTON; high school; parochial schools.

WATERLOO, near Liverpool; high school; parochial school.

WIGAN; high school; school for pupil-teachers; parochial schools.

Notre Dame, Poor School Sisters of (of the German Institute).

Founded in 1833 at Ratisbon, Bavaria, by the Bishop, Mgr. Wittmann, and Father Sebastian Job, with the coöperation of Caroline Gerhardinger. The Rule is that of the Blessed Pierre Fourier, for a Congregation founded in Lorraine in the seventeenth century, with suitable modifications, and approved by Pius IX. The object of the Institution is, besides the sanctification of its own members, the education of female youth. They are under the jurisdiction of the Bishop.

Has many houses on the Continent and in America. Mother House at Munich. The Community is governed by a Mother-General and assistants, assisted by the Father Spiritual, residing at Munich. There are several provincial mother-houses, to which training colleges are attached for the province.

Vows.—The three usual vows, with a fourth one of devotion to "the instruction and education of girls."

Habit.—Black, with black mantle, white guimpe and bandeau, and black veil.

Introduced into England in 1864 by Canon Purcell.

BIRMINGHAM, Broad Street; St. Peter's Government School.

SOUTHEND-ON-SEA, St. Mary's Convent; Orphanage; founded by Cardinal Wiseman.

WOOLWICH, 2 Nightingale Vale; middle schools.

Notre Dame des Missions, Nuns of.

Object.—English and French education.

CANTERBURY, Westbere.

DEAL, West Street; boarding-school; Orphanage; day-school.

Notre Dame de Sion, Daughters of.

Founded by Alphonse and Théodore Ratisbonne; and approved by Pius IX. in May 1848. The Sisters devote themselves principally to the charge and education of Jewish children and converts, but also undertake the education of girls generally, especially Poor Schools and Orphanages. Unite the active with the contemplative life.

Vows.—Take the three simple vows, at first annually for five years, and then for five years. After ten years these may be taken for life. Mother House at Paris; and they have several Convents in the Holy Land and in Syria: the largest of these is at Jerusalem.

LONDON:

Bayswater, W., Convent, Our Lady of Sion, Sion House, 17, 18, 19, and 20 Powis Square; upper-class boarding and day school for young ladies; also a middle school for day-scholars and a preparatory school for little boys.

HOLLOWAY, N., Eden Grove; boarding and day school; lady boarders.

WORTHING; boarding-school for young ladies.

Paul, Sisters of St.

COSSEY, Norwich.

CUMNOCK, N.B.

DANESFIELD, Bucks.

GREAT MARLOW, Bucks.

Peace of St. Joseph, Sisters of.

GREAT GRIMSBY, Lincolnshire.

NOTTINGHAM, Blue Bell Hill.

Perpetual Adoration, Sisters of the Blessed Sacrament, or Sacramentines.

Founded in 1639 at Marseilles, by Ven. Père Antoine Lequieu, of the Order of St. Dominic. Approved by Innocent XI., and confirmed by Innocent XII. Erected by the latter into a religious Order in 1693. Introduced into England in 1863 by the Bishop of Clifton, the Right Rev. Dr. Clifford—the first establishment

INSTITUTE OF ADORATION.

of the Order being under Rev. Mother Emélie Pellier, at Cannington, near Bristol, whence the Community have since removed to their present abode at Taunton.

Object.—Perpetual day and night adoration of the Blessed Sacrament, including the work of reparation and intercession.

Rule of St. Augustine, adapted. Contemplative. Enclosed. Lay associates, who, living in the world, obtain a share in the merit of the good works of the Order by devoting themselves to a certain hour of adoration each year.

Habit of black serge, with white scapular, veil, and cloak. Over the heart, and on the right arm, is worn a silver medal, representing the Blessed Sacrament.

TAUNTON, Somerset.

Perpetual Adoration, Institute of.

Founded in 1843, in Belgium, by some pious ladies, aided by Père Boone, S.J. Enriched with indulgences by Leo XIII.

The objects of the Association are—(1) To make Jesus Christ in the Blessed Sacrament of the Altar known, loved, and perpetually adored; and to make reparation for the outrages to the Blessed Sacrament. (2) To help those poor churches which are destitute of the requisites for divine worship both at home and among the heathen. Seculars are admitted as associates in these works.

MANCHESTER, St. Gertrude's House, 28 Alexandra Park.

Perpetual Adoration of the Blessed Sacrament, Irish Sisters of.

Founded in October 1874, under Right Rev. Dr. Furlong, Bishop of Ferns.

Objects.—Perpetual day and night adoration of the Blessed Sacrament; religious instruction and preparation for Communion; spiritual retreats for ladies; making of vestments, &c.

Rule of St. Ignatius, adapted.

WEXFORD, Convent of Perpetual Adoration.

Poor Child Jesus, Sisters of the.

A German Order, exiled from Prussia by the May Laws. Cloistered; devoted to care and education of poor children.

RUGBY, Southam, Convent of Poor Child Jesus.

Poor Clares or Minoresses, of the Second Order of St. Francis.

Founded by St. Francis in 1212, and received its name from its first Abbess, St. Clare of Assisi. Approved by Innocent IV. in 1246.

Rule of St. Francis, the strict poverty of which being mitigated at one time by Urban IV., those who follow the latter Rule are called Urbanists. In 1436 St. Colette instituted a reform, by which the original strictness of the Rule was upheld; these Poor Clares are called Poor Clare Colettines.

Habit.—Formerly gray, now brown, with a cord round the waist, and a cloak during ceremonies in church.

Introduced into England in 1293. Dispersed at Dissolution. First English house reëstablished at Gravelines in 1609, from which filiations came to Ireland in 1625. At the French Revolution all the English Nuns came to England, and are now represented by the Poor Clares, Clare Abbey, Darlington. The Poor Clare Colettines came to England from Bruges in 1850, and their Convents are now in the majority here. The extern lay Sisters live outside the enclosure, in order to transact the necessary business of the Convent. They observe the Rule of the Third Order Regular of St. Francis, and, besides their ordinary duties, they often teach the Poor School, and visit the poor and sick.

ARUNDEL, Sussex (Colettines). Founded by the Duchess of Norfolk, 1886.

BADDESLEY-CLINTON, Knowle, Warwickshire (Colettines). Founded from Bruges, 1850, in a building which had formerly been a Franciscan College. The extern Sisters teach a Poor School and visit the poor and sick.

BULLINGHAM, Hereford.

DARLINGTON, St. Clare's Abbey. Represents Gravelines and its filiations. After some wanderings, finally settled here in 1857.

DUNBLANE, N.B. (Colettines).

MANCHESTER, Alma Park, Levenshulme (Colettines). Founded from Bruges, 1863. Extern Sisters have care of parish church and school.

LONDON, Cornwall Road, Notting Hill, Convent of Sacred Heart of Jesus (Colettines). Founded in 1857 by Cardinal Manning from Bruges.

YORK, Laurence Street, St. Joseph's Convent (Colettines).

BALLYJAMESDUFF, Cavan, Convent founded in 1872 from Cavan; day-schools.

CAVAN, Convent founded in 1861 from Harold's Cross and Newry; certified Industrial school of St. Joseph, and large day-schools.

DUBLIN, Convent, Harold's Cross, where the Nuns have resided since 1803, having previously, in 1712, removed from Galway to Dorset Street, Dublin. Primary school and female orphanage. At the latter institution, the girls (born of respectable parents who have fallen into poverty) are maintained, clothed, educated, and ultimately provided for by the Nuns. At the request of one of the former Archbishops of Dublin, Benedict XIV. and Pius

VII. mitigated the original severity of the Rule, and modified it, so as to enable the Nuns to devote themselves to the education of poor children, for whom Catholic education had been almost an impossibility until the commencement of the present century.

GALWAY. Founded from Dublin and Athlone in 1652. The Poor Clares in Galway are subject to the Roman General and Father Provincial of the Irish Province; they are the only ones in Ireland under the Order. Galway is the parent house of all the Irish Poor Clares. All the branch houses commuted part of their Rule for teaching, and are under the jurisdiction of Bishops, who obtained the permission from Rome. These Nuns are very anxious to resume their enclosure if means permitted.

KEADY, Co. Armagh (Convent founded in 1871 from Newry); day-school and night-school for factory girls.

KENMARE, Killarney, Co. Kerry (founded 1861 by the sister of Lord O'Hagan); large primary schools, where over four hundred children are gratuitously taught; lace-school, where poor girls are taught lace-making.

NEWRY (founded 1830 by the Bishop of Dromore from Harold's Cross, Dublin). Owing to the want of Catholic education at the time, these Nuns, as well as other contemplative Orders, were obliged to take charge of orphans and large day-schools, which necessitated some alteration of the primitive Rule, such as the constant fasts and other austerities.

VIRGINIA, Co. Cavan (founded from Newry).

Poor Handmaids of Jesus Christ.

Object.—Devotion to the poor and sick poor.

HENDON, Middlesex, N.W., Convent of St. Joseph.

LONDON, Whitechapel, E., Convent, 17 Mulberry Street; German schools and nursing the German sick.

Poor Servants of the Mother of God and Servants of the Poor.

This Institute was founded by the late Lady Georgiana Fullerton in the year 1868. Its object is to render as much service as possible to the poor, and, in order to do so, to make the houses of the Institute self-supporting; and in many places the Sisters undertake laundry, needlework, &c., for this purpose. Their Constitutions are founded on those of St. Ignatius, with modifications. Their Mother House is in Rome, 16 Via San Sebastianello, Piazza de Spagna.

BRENTFORD, Middlesex; visitation of the poor, and classes for Catechism.

LONDON, 3 Green Court, Little Pulteney Street, Soho; visitation of the poor of several missions; classes for Catechism; instruction of adults and converts; Refuge for fallen women, where they can be immediately received, and afterwards passed on to the houses of the Good Shepherd and other Catholic asylums.

NORTH HYDE, Middlesex; Infirmary for boys of the Poor Law school.

ROEHAMPTON, S.W.; Orphanage for girls.

ST. HELENS, Lancashire; visitation of the poor; a night-school for collier lads; public free Hospital for men, women, and children.

CARRIGTUOHILL, Co. Cork; national schools; visit of the poor; care of different sodalities.

Nazareth (Poor Sisters of).

Founded by Cardinal Wiseman in 1851.

The Sisters of this Congregation follow the Rule of St. Augustine, and are under the immediate authority of the Holy See. The Mother House (with Noviceship) is situated at Hammersmith in the archdiocese, and no lay Sisters are received.

The object of this Congregation is to find a home for the aged poor of both sexes (who are received irrespective of creed), and for orphan, destitute, infirm, and incurable children (but those entirely idiotic or suffering from epileptic fits are not admitted). Food is also given at the door to poor people, wounds dressed, and medicine given when necessary.

POOR SISTERS OF NAZARETH.

For the support of the poor, the Sisters depend entirely on the alms, food, and clothing which they collect from house to house; and in giving these alms Protestants are particularly generous.

LONDON, Hammersmith, Nazareth House; Mother House and Novitiate, built at a cost of more than 40,000*l*., chiefly contributed by the Sisters, and which can accommodate 400 poor. The following are the branch houses of the Congregation:

CUPARSTONE, Aberdeen, Nazareth House.

CARDIFF, Wales, North Road, Nazareth House.

CHELTENHAM, St. James's Square, Nazareth House.

MIDDLESBROUGH, Albert Park, Nazareth House.

NORTHAMPTON, Nazareth House.

NOTTINGHAM, Priory Street, Lenton, Nazareth House, built on the site and of the stones of Lenton Priory, which was founded in 1086.

OXFORD, Cowley Road, Nazareth House.

SOUTHEND, Essex, Nazareth House.

SOUTHSEA, Hants, Wilson Grove, Nazareth House.

BELFAST, Ballynafeigh, Nazareth House.

Presentation (of our Blessed Lady in the Temple), Nuns of the.

Founded 1776, at Cork, by Miss Honora Nagle, who, at the same time and place, instituted an Asylum for aged women, having previously established a Convent of Ursulines. Approved by Pius VI., 3rd September 1791; confirmed as a religious Order by Pius VII., 9th April 1805.

Object.—The gratuitous instruction of the female poor; take charge also of Industrial schools and Orphanages. Introduced into England, at Manchester, in 1836.

Rule of St. Ursula. Vows of chastity, poverty, obedience, and perseverance in the work of charitable Catholic education. Enclosure. Subject to Bishop of diocese.

MANCHESTER, Convent, Livesey Street (founded from Clonmel in 1836 by Mr. Patrick Lavery); large girls' and infant schools; Orphanage for girls.

BAGENALSTOWN, Co. Carlow.

BALLINGARRY, Co. Limerick (Glenview).

BALTINGLASS, Co. Wicklow.

BANDON, Co. Cork (founded 1829); national schools; school for little boys.

CAHIRCIVEEN, Co. Kerry.

CARLOW.

CARRICK-ON-SUIR, Co. Tipperary, with

schools. Destitute children are fed and clothed in winter.

CASHEL, Co. Tipperary, with Orphanage and certified school (Industrial).

CASTLECOMER, Co. Kilkenny (founded 1849 from Kilkenny).

CASTLETOWN.

CASTLEISLAND, Co. Kerry.

CLANE, Naas.

CLONDALKIN, Co. Dublin, Convent of the Immaculate Conception; school for young ladies; Poor Schools.

CLONMEL, Co. Tipperary, with schools.

CORK, South, with Asylum for aged women; parent house of Order (founded 1777).

CORK, North, Convent, Clarence Street (founded 1779).

CROSSHAVEN, Cork, St. Bridgid's.

DINGLE, Tralee, Co. Kerry.

DONERAILE, Buttevant, Co. Cork; schools.

DROGHEDA; large day and Sunday school for poor children and adults, many of whom are fed and clothed.

DUBLIN:

George's Hill (1790); schools for poor children and orphans.

Terenure, St. Joseph's; schools.

DUNGARVAN, Co. Waterford, with large schools (founded 1809). Destitute children fed and clothed.

ENNISCORTHY, Co. Wexford.

FERMOY, Co. Cork, Convent of St. Joseph; schools.

FETHARD, Clonmel, Co. Tipperary.

GALWAY.

KILCOCK, Co. Kildare; Foreign Mission Novitiate.

KILDARE.

KILKENNY.

KILLARNEY, Co. Kerry.

LIMERICK; schools for girls and infant boys.

LISMORE, Co. Waterford; schools (founded 1836). The late and present Dukes of Devonshire gave land and support.

LISTOWEL, Co. Kerry.

LIXNAW, Co. Limerick, New Bethlehem (founded 1877).

LUCAN, Co. Dublin (founded 1867); Poor Schools; middle schools. Provide situations for orphan girls and others.

MARYBOROUGH, Queen's Co.

MAYNOOTH, Co. Kildare; schools (founded 1823).

MIDLETON, Co. Cork; schools.

MILLSTREET, Co. Cork.

MILLTOWN, Co. Kerry (founded 1824).

MITCHELSTOWN, Co. Cork; schools.

MOONCOIN, Co. Waterford.

MOUNTMELLICK, Queen's Co.

MULLINGAR, Co. Westmeath.

ORANMORE, Co. Galway.

PORTADOWN, Armagh (opened 1882; first branch in Ulster); day, night, and Sunday schools.

PORTARLINGTON.

RAHAN, Tullamore (founded 1817).

RATHMORE, Kerry.

SNEEM, Co. Kerry.

STRADBALLY, Queen's Co.

TRALEE, Co. Kerry.

THURLES, Co. Tipperary, with a certified Industrial school and Orphanage.

TUAM, Co. Galway; 300 poor girls gratuitously educated, taught needlework, and apprenticed to trades, the more destitute being fed and clothed.

WATERFORD, schools.

WEXFORD.

YOUGHAL, Co. Cork; schools.

Providence of the Immaculate Conception (Sisters of).

Founded in 1833 at Champion, diocese of Namur, by Monsignor the Canon Jean Baptiste Victor Kinet.

Objects.—Education and the direction of Hospitals, Asylums, Prisons, Orphanages, &c. Mother House at Champion.

Rule.—Special.

LONDON, Hampstead, N.W., Convent of Providence, Hampstead Green; middle-class boarding and day schools, and a special department for female infants of widowed gentlemen; Poor Law school for girls, certified by Government.

Redemptoristines (Nuns of the Most Holy Redeemer).

Founded at La Scala about 1731 by St. Alphonsus Liguori, in connection with the Redemptorist Fathers, the latter imitating the active, while the Nuns imitate the hidden, life of our Lord. They are strictly contemplative. The Sisters chant the Divine Office.

From Italy the Order spread to Austria, Belgium, Holland, and France; and in 1859 Cardinal Cullen invited them to Ireland.

Solemn vows of poverty, chastity, and obedience, and one of perpetual enclosure.

Habit consists of a red tunic, in honour of the Passion of our Lord; a blue mantle and scapular, to which is attached a picture of our most Holy Redeemer; and the rosary of fifteen decades, with a large medal of the instruments of the Passion.

Dublin, Fairview, Monastery of St. Alphonsus.

Retreat of the Sacred Heart of Jesus. (Sisters of).

Founded 1682, at Quimper, by Mother Teresa of Hernieno, assisted by Père Huby, S.J. Introduced into England 1882.

Objects.—1. To promote the glory of God and the reign of the Sacred Heart by the work of retreats. These retreats are either general or private.

2. To train up young ladies of the upper and middle classes.

3. To keep Poor Schools when and where required.

4. To undertake pious works in keeping with the principal object of the Institute.

Any person wishing to live a retired life may be received as a lady boarder.

Rule of the Society of Jesus, suitably adapted to its purpose.

Habit.—Black. They wear a silver heart as an emblem of their devotion to the Sacred Heart of Jesus.

Leo XIII., by his Brief, so favourable to the Institute, has granted it several plenary and partial indulgences.

SUMMERFIELD, Granville Road, Sevenoaks, Kent; boarding-school for young ladies; lady boarders; private retreats.

Most Holy Sacrament (Nuns of the).

Founded in 1715 at Boncieu-le-Roi, Ardèche, France, by Père Vigne.

Objects.—Female education of the rich and poor; care of hospitals, &c.

Rule of St. Augustine.

LONDON, the Convent, 35 Brompton Square, S.W.; boarding and day-boarding school for young ladies of the higher classes; preparatory schools for young gentlemen from five to ten years of age.

Sacré Cœur de Jesus (Sacred Heart of Jesus), Nuns of the.

Founded in 1800 by Madame Madeline Sophie Barat.

Object.—The higher education of young ladies, the Convents having also Poor Schools and Orphanages attached to them, and spiritual retreats for ladies. Mother House at 77 Rue de Varennes, Paris.

Rule of St. Ignatius.

Habit.—Black, with white muslin cap.

BRIGHTON, West, Sussex, Convent of the Sacred Heart, The Drive, Cliftonville; boarding-school for young ladies. Course of studies as at Roehampton.

ROEHAMPTON, Surrey, Convent of the Sacré Cœur; boarding-school for young ladies of the higher class; gratuitous instruction of the poor.

WANDSWORTH, Surrey, Convent of the Sacred Heart, West Hill, S.W.; training school for pupil-teachers and other young persons who have completed their eighteenth year, to be prepared as teachers in elementary schools under Government inspectors.

ARMAGH, Convent of the Sacré Cœur; first-class boarding and day school for young ladies; free school for poor female children of the city.

DUBLIN:
18 Lower Leeson Street, Convent of the Sacred Heart; school for young ladies.

Mount Anville, Dundrum, Convent of the Sacred Heart; education of young ladies; instruction of the poor; private retreats at any time, and three general retreats a year for ladies.

ROSCREA, Convent of the Sacred Heart; boarding-school for young ladies.

Sacred Heart of Jesus (Servants of the).

Founded in 1866 in Paris, by Rev. Père Victor Braun, and have been since introduced into England.

Objects.—All works for the spiritual and bodily benefit of the poor and working classes of all creeds; visiting and nursing them, whatever their diseases; supplying them with comforts and tending their children; looking after and instructing factory and other girls; directing Hospitals and Prison Infirmaries; providing Orphanages; Asylums for the aged poor of both sexes, &c. In England the Sisters accept the direction of day-schools attached to the missions. Mother House at Versailles; Provincial House and Novitiate in London.

Rule of St. Augustine, with adapted constitutions. Are consecrated in a special manner to the service of the Sacred Heart of Jesus. Vows at first annual, afterwards perpetual. Under the patronage of St. Francis of Sales; and, for the novices, of Blessed Margaret Mary.

ABERDARE, Glamorgan.

CHIDEOCK, near Bridport, Co. Dorset; Poor Schools.

CUMNOCK, N.B., Cottage Hospital, founded 1882, and supported by the Marquis of Bute.

HOMERTON, Middlesex, Convent, Sydney House, Hassett Road, E. (Provincial House in England); novitiate, Orphanage for girls, day-school, and evening sewing-class in winter for young women. The Sisters teach the schools at Upper Clapton, Mile End, Kingsland, and Homerton, where they also visit the poor and sick.

LLANARTH, Raglan, Co. Monmouth; Poor Schools; visitation of sick and poor.

LONDON, 16 Leicester Square and 10 Leicester Place, W.C. Charge of the French Hospital and Dispensary, 10 Leicester Place and 40 Lister Street, Leicester Square; and of the school and Asile de Notre Dame de France, 16 Leicester Square.

ROTHESAY, N.B.

MERTHYR TYDVIL.

Sacred Hearts of Jesus and Mary (Sisters of).

Education of the poor, and other works of charity.

SPENNYMOOR, Durham, The Tudhoe Home, Tudhoe; diocesan certified Poor Law school for Catholic children from the workhouse.

Sacred Heart of Mary (Sisters of the).

Founded in 1848 at Berziers, diocese of Montpellier, by Père Gailhac, assisted by Madame Cure. Introduced into Ireland, at Lisburn, in 1870; and into England, at Bootle, in 1873. Mother House at Berziers.

Object.—Female education of all classes.

Rule of St. Augustine, adapted. Vows of poverty, chastity, obedience, and zeal, taken for five years, and then for life.

Habit of blue serge, with coif and guimpe of white linen under a long black veil, for choir Sisters, and of black for lay Sisters; silver cross and heart on breast.

LIVERPOOL, Convent, Seafield House, Seaforth (1873); boarding-school for the higher education of young ladies, and day and Poor Schools; also elementary schools of St. James, Bootle, and Blessed Sacrament, Walton.

FERRYBANK, Waterford; school for young ladies; Poor Schools.

LISBURN, near Belfast (1870); large boarding-school for young ladies; Poor Schools.

Sainte - Union des Sacres Cœurs (Sisters of).

Founded in 1828 at Douai, by Very Rev. Jean Baptiste Debrabant, of the diocese of Cambrai. Introduced into England in 1859.

Object.—The education of girls in every rank of society.

Rule drawn up by the founder; taken chiefly from Rule of the Visitation, by St. Francis de Sales.

BATH, Convent, Pulteney Road; boarding-school for young ladies; preparatory school for boys of six to nine years of age; Poor Schools.

ERITH, Kent, Convent, Bexley Road; receive young ladies as boarders; weekly boarders and day pupils.

LONDON:

Lilford House, Highgate Road, N.W.; weekly boarding and day school for young ladies.

Loreto Villa, Junction Road, Upper Holloway; day-school for young ladies; preparatory school for boys of six to nine years of age.

SOUTHAMPTON, Archer's Lodge; boarding-school for young ladies; preparatory school for boys.

Servites, Nuns (of the Third Order) or Servants of Mary.

Founded towards the close of the thirteenth century at Florence, by St. Juliana Falconieri, under the direction of her uncle, Blessed Alexis, who was one of the seven founders of the Servite Order. Established in England 1864.

Objects.—Education of the rich and poor, and the care of Orphanages, workrooms, the sick and poor, &c.; and special propagation of the devotion to Our Lady of the Seven Dolours.

Rule of St. Augustine, with additional constitutions approved by Martin V.

Habit.—A black tunic and scapular of the Seven Dolours, plaited linen wimple and black veil (lined with white, and showing white border), leathern belt round the waist, and rosary of the Seven Dolours; crucifix worn in front under the scapular, on which, over the heart, is an image of the Sacred Host, in memory of the miracle which took place at the death of St. Juliana. In choir, and when going out, the Nuns wear a large black mantle, covering the head and coming down to the feet, whence they are called *Mantellate*, to distinguish them from the Second Order. The professed wear a gold ring.

ARUNDEL, Sussex; education of the poor.

LONDON, Stamford Hill, N., Convent, St. Mary's Priory, St. Anne's Road (Mother House); boarding-school for a small number of young ladies. And at Le Raincy, near Paris, and Cuves, Haute Marne, France.

Teresa, St., Tertiaries of (of the Third Order of Carmel).

WARDOUR CASTLE, Wilts, Convent of St. Mary.

Ursuline Nuns.

Founded in 1535 at Brescia, in Italy, by St. Angela of Merici, and named after Ursula, an English Saint of the fifth century. Approved by Paul III. as a religious Congregation in 1544, and by Gregory XIII. as an Order in 1572. Established in Paris by Madame de St. Beuve in 1604; and in Ireland, at Cork, 18th September 1771, by Miss Honora Nagle, foundress of the Presentation Order. Introduced into England at Upton, near Stratford.

Object.—Education of the better classes; the Convents of the Order having also attached to them schools for poor girls. In establishing the Ursulines at Cork, Miss Nagle was the means of practically restoring conventualism to Ireland, the Ursuline being the first Convent openly founded there since the Reformation.

Rule of St. Augustine. Enclosed.

LONDON:

Blackheath, S.E., Convent of Our Lady Star of the Sea (from Hanover), Croom's Hill.

48 Lee Park, Convent of St. Joseph (branch of preceding).

Boarding-schools for young ladies at both Convents.

UPTON, Convent, Forest Gate, Essex; boarding-school for young ladies; day-school for children of the middle class.

CORK, Couvent at Blackrock (1825); school for young ladies.

SLIGO; boarding and day schools.

THURLES, Co. Tipperary (1787); superior boarding-school for young ladies; day-schools; Poor Schools.

WATERFORD (1815); founded from Thurles.

Ursulines of Jesus (Dames de Chavagnes).

Founded in 1802 at Chavagnes, Vendée, by Rev. Louis Marie Baudouin, assisted by Madame Ranfray de la Rochette. Introduced in 1834 into Scotland by the late Right Rev. Dr. Gillis, Bishop of the Eastern District, who, in founding the Convent of St. Margaret, Edinburgh, established the first religious house in North Britain since the dissolution.

Objects.—Female education of the upper and middle classes, as well as religious and general instruction in Poor Schools; visiting the poor and sick, &c.

Rule of St. Augustine, with adaptations from that of St. Ignatius. Under control of the diocesan.

EDINBURGH, N.B., Convent of St. Margaret; boarding-school for the higher education of young ladies.

PERTH, N.B., Convent of St. Joseph (1866); instruction of Catholic female prisoners in the general prison; in charge of Poor Schools; visit the poor and sick.

SWANSEA, Glamorganshire, Convent of St. Mary and St. Winefride; boarding-school for the French and English education of young ladies; girls' and infant schools.

Ursula, St. (Sisters of).

STOWMARKET, Suffolk; Convent, and boarding-school for young ladies.

Visitation (Nuns of the).

Founded in 1610 at Annecy, in Savoy, by St. Francis de Sales and St. Jane Frances Frémiot, Baroness de Chantal. The Order is contemplative and enclosed, but many of the Convents have schools for young ladies.

The intention of the founder was that those persons should be received into his Congregation who, through weak health or advanced age, were unable to enter the other religious Orders in which great austerity of life was practised. But he requires that, to supply for these austerities, his Religious should excel in the virtues of humility, charity, and interior mortification.

It was to a Nun of this Order—Blessed Margaret Mary Alacoque—that the devotion to the Sacred Heart was revealed.

Rule of St. Augustine, with constitutions of St. Francis de Sales.*

Introduced into England at Acton House, London, in 1804, by Mrs. Tunstall of Wycliffe Hall, Yorks. Removed first to Shepton Mallet, and finally, in 1831, to

WESTBURY-ON-TRYM, Convent of Visitation.

WALMER, Kent, Convent of Visitation, Roselands. Founded 1875 by the expelled Nuns from the Convents of Himmelsthür, Hildesheim, and Ostrowo, Posen. Superior boarding-school.

* *Life of St. Francis of Sales*, by Hamon. *Life of St. Jane Frances de Chantal.* (London: Burns & Oates.)

www.ingramcontent.com/pod-product-compliance
Lightning Source LLC
Chambersburg PA
CBHW021013240426
43669CB00037B/933